Foreword

Twenty-five years ago Britain's C(war, not in Europe where it had lived, trained and prepared itself for the meltdown with the Warsaw Pact, but in the open deserts of northern Saudi Arabia, southern Iraq and Kuwait. The Gulf War of 1991 was unique, particularly when viewed from the perspective of the bloody but inconclusive wars which Britain has recently fought in Afghanistan – and again, in Iraq. For a start it was a coalition war with limited objectives which achieved conclusive strategic success; Kuwait was liberated and Saddam Hussein's massive Iraqi army decisively and humiliatingly defeated. Moreover, a coalition which not only included old allies such as the US and Britain, but also less familiar bed fellows such as Egypt and Syria held together. Such unity of purpose is remarkable when viewed from today's perspective. Next, from a military perspective, the Gulf War of 1991 was the last great tank battle of the 20th Century, perhaps of any century. Britain sent a division of two brigades, an artillery brigade and almost the entire logistic capability of 1st British Corps to fight a truly joined up air/land battle. Given cuts to defence capability by successive governments over the past two decades, such an achievement would be impossible today. Finally, to those who took part, it was 'our' war. While the combat was short lived and the casualties thankfully very light, it was nevertheless a unique experience of major combat operations which formed lasting bonds between those who fought which have stood the test of time.

'Challenging the Beast' tells the story of that war from the perspective of a tank troop leader and offers a unique insight into the challenges faced by junior commanders. It is above all a story of the comradeship of the tank crew and shines a powerful light on the qualities and humour of the cavalry soldiers of the 14th/20th King's Hussars whose story this is. In writing this book John Dingley has done those soldiers a great service.

General Sir Richard Shirreff KCB CBE

(formerly 'B' Squadron Leader, 14th/20th King's Hussars)

Challenging The Beast

A Junior Officer's memoires of a Tank Troop
in the Gulf War 1990-91
The 4th Armoured Brigade (The Forgotten Brigade)

Authors note:

I have always wanted to write this book to have a record for my sons on what Daddy did in his war and for the members of my Troop, Squadron and Regiment who might enjoy it for their sons and daughters. I am far from being a Shakespeare or even an Andy McNab, in fact I am slightly dyslexic, and so writing does not come easily to me. So I apologise if the prose is poor and the sentence construction clumsy, but this is the story of my troop, 2nd Troop, B Squadron, 14th/20th Kings Hussars during the Gulf War of 1990-91. I also wanted to capture some of the more mundane aspects of being on operations, the things not spoken about in other books, so I apologise if you are slightly taken aback by some things we had to do…
I did not keep a diary during the war, but have my notebooks from Orders Groups (O-groups) and most importantly my scrapbook of photos that I completed in 1993 when my memory was far fresher than it is now. I have used the pictures from my scrapbook in the form of scans of the actual scrapbook as I feel it adds to the feelings of the 1990's. I have also placed the pictures in the body of the text as I strongly believe that a picture paints a thousand words and the context is better kept than when the photos are grouped in the centre of the book as so often is the case. As a result, not all the incidents and goings on are necessarily in chronological order, but most are. For the actual fighting, I used the B Squadron Battle write up done by Major Richard Shirreff published in the book 'Iron Fist', which covers the major historical engagements of tanks since their debut in 1916. This along with Robert Fox's article from the Telegraph Magazine published after the

war has ensured that the actual battle sequences are in order however some of the anecdotal stories may be slightly adrift.

I am also eternally grateful to my father-in-law, Nick Paterson who had the unenviable task of doing the first edit and Simon Brady who did the second edit. I also indebted to the Regimental website members who have helped with the odd 'grey matter' jogging. I should also thank the UN for my posting to Juba in South Sudan where I found time to start and the UN Security System for making ample time for me to write this while on 'lock-down' in Sanaa during the most recent troubles in Yemen.

El Fasher, Darfur
Sudan
2015.

Table of Contents

List of Pictures and illustrations:

Dedication

This book is dedicated to Lieutenant Edward Whitehead 16th/5th Lancers and those who lost their lives in the service of their country in the liberation of Kuwait and those who still suffer for their service.

And for all those who 'marched off the square' too soon
Sergeant Major 'Skip' Rae 14th/20th Kings Hussars
Lance Corporal Stu Lythgoe 14th/20th Kings Hussars

REGIMENTAL COLLECT

Almighty God, by whose power and in whose mercy we are shielded from danger and pardoned when we have done wrong, help us all, as members of the 14th/20th King's Hussars, to find in our service in the Regiment a sure way of serving thee, help us to dedicate our lives in that we may live for others rather than ourselves, and grant that through the power of the Holy Spirit we may be steadfast in duty, patient in hardship, and bold at all times to declare the truth in the name of him who loves us and died for us. Jesus Christ Our Lord.

Also to my sister Lois

Map of Operation Desert Sabre

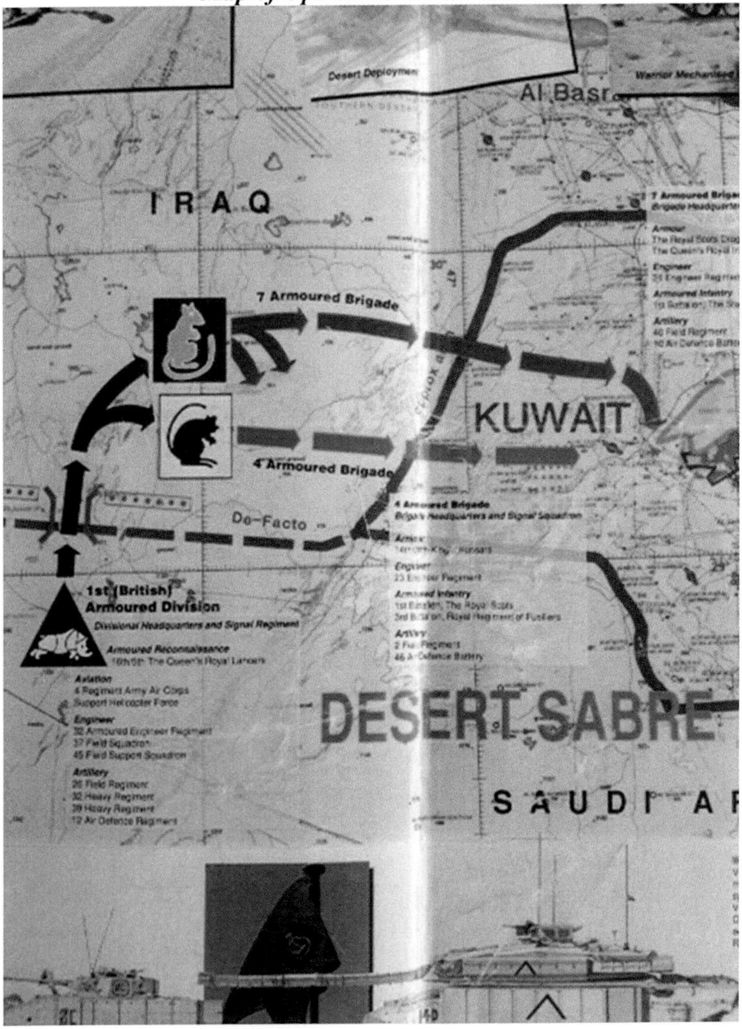

Introduction.

It is 25 years since I took part in the 'Great' Gulf War as some of us veterans of this war term it. It was the last conclusive victory that the British Army has taken part in recent times and is possibly the last major divisional armoured confrontation that the British Army is likely to have. It is also a war that had sound justification and this mattered a great deal for the soldiers sent on the ultimate mission, the one we had trained for, the one we feared, the one we never expected to perform. There were some who relished the chance to test their mettle against the world's fourth biggest army. In my Regiment, Squadron and Troop this was not a common emotion or feeling. Most of us were prepared for this test; we were almost to a man confident we could carry ourselves in the traditions of the Regiment and the British Army. I think we felt confident that we would overcome but did not know what the cost would be. I certainly feared that it would be high and chemical weapons might be used resulting in massive casualties. In my mind I was prepared if necessary to take over as the Squadron Leader or worse commanding the Regiment. However in my heart I was sure in that we would prevail.

Acknowledgements

Special thanks to Nick Paterson for dealing with his dyslexic son-in-law's ramblings and my boss in Sudan, Simon Brady for his patience in improving my composition. I also want to thank my darling wife Katrina for her support and help in doing the final proof reading while suffering a posting in Khartoum. Finally my father, Richard Dingley who proofed the printed version.

I wish also to thank Robert Fox for his article published in the Sunday Telegraph Magazine that helped me keep things in the right order.

Chapter 1
From 'Troubled Province' to War

I had just returned from a long rural patrol in Northern Ireland when I heard that Sadam Hussein had invaded Kuwait. Jerry Denning and Simon Graham my fellow Troop Leaders were sitting watching the news in the port-a-cabin that served as the officers' mess in Longkesh Camp just outside the walls of the Maze Prison.

We sat watching and discussing the event realising that our being in Northern Ireland meant we would almost certainly miss out on any British deployment to the Gulf.
Our worst fears were realised a few days later when we were told that 7th Armoured Brigade had just been put on notice to move to Saudi Arabia as part of Operation Desert Shield. I had mixed feelings of relief and also envy of those guys destined to go. Within days we heard that a troop from 14th / 20th Kings Hussars was to join the Royal Scots Dragoon Guards (RSDG) who formed one of the two armoured regiments of 7th Armoured Brigade.
A good friend, Alistair Todd known by all as 'Ron' Todd after the then active trades union leader was to lead this group of soldiers and fill the role as squadron battle captain, along with other troops of various regiments to supplement the under manned RSDG squadrons. These troops came from D Squadron. Their Squadron Leader, Charles Clarke had a number of misgivings. Firstly, his boys were not going as a formed unit, so might lose their regimental identity, and he would not be leading them. Concerns I felt were justified but not particularly well received by some at Regimental Headquarters.

As the build-up continued and the press speculated we continued patrolling in places such as South Armagh, West Belfast, Londonderry and the New Barnsley area above Belfast. Over in Northern Ireland HQ (HQNI) sat a good regimental friend of ours, Henry Joynson. He had taken up a post prior to our deployment as a watch keeper at HQNI in order to 'get his medal' and also break out of the humdrum life in Germany. Henry called us on an almost daily basis asking for news and whether 4th Armoured Brigade had been 'stood to' to go. Jerry Denning decided a good wind up on Henry was in order…

The mess waiter came in to say that Captain Joynson was on the phone, and that he wished to speak with any of the officers. Jerry took the phone, "Hi Henry, can't talk as we are in a mad rush packing," [Henry]: 'What, why?", [Jerry]: Because last night Richard got a signal that it is 4th Armoured Brigade that is going to the Gulf to join 7th Armoured", [Henry]: 'Bugger, crap, when are you shipping out?" [Jerry]: Not sure yet but may be tomorrow, but certainly before the end of the week". [Henry]: "Who is taking over from you?" [Jerry]: 42 Plant Squadron RE have been pulled off their NITAT (Northern Ireland Tactical Advanced Training) course early and deploying". [Henry]: OK, speak to you later…

Within the hour we got a call from the Adjutant in Germany telling us to stop winding up Henry, as he had called the Commanding Officer, his boss in HQNI and was just about to call the Commander of Northern Ireland begging to shorten his assignment as a watch keeper to join the Regiment in the Gulf deployment!

The summer continued and the build-up in Saudi was of much interest to us all but the pressure of our job kept our minds focused on our present operational role. The Squadron carried out a number of tasks in its role as The Maze Prison Guard Force (PGF). We patrolled the local area around the prison, which also included the village of Hillsborough, an extremely loyalist area with many civil servants and well-heeled families. These patrols reminded me of country walks back in England after a pub lunch on a Sunday. We would often patrol through wonderful gardens of stately homes and be offered tea by extremely nice and understanding people.

The second task was in comparison far less pleasant, that of patrolling Lisburn town, the home of HQNI. This ostensibly loyalist town had been the scene of a number of IRA atrocities over the Troubles because of its strong loyalist population, but also as the home of the British Army in Northern Ireland. As a result, the PGF provided a surge or extra capacity at night and patrolled from 6pm to 6am every night with three mobile patrols of two armoured Land Rovers each. This was without doubt the worst task as it involved long nights and little positive reaction from the local population. We did however manage to have some fun. Like one morning when deploying a Vehicle Check Point (VCP) on the back road from Aldergrove Airport I stopped a car with a family of four inside. I politely asked for the driver's identity document and as he got it out I apologised for stopping them and made small talk.... I asked where they were coming from, whereupon the wife answered the airport, "oh" I said, "have you been on holiday" as I noticed they were quite sunburned. "Yes" came the reply, "Majorca". I then asked which flight and hotel and took a mental note of the information before sending them on their way with my usual cheery 'sorry for delaying you' phrase. A few minutes later a second car came up the road and we flagged it down, in side was a family of four all looking sunburned, so I put two and two together and asked for the drivers ID. Once I got it I identified Mr David MacManus (not his real name) and asked, "Did you have a good holiday in Majorca Mr MacManus?" He looked at me in stunned disbelief, I then asked what he felt about the 'Hotel de la Vila' was it nice? He stammered that it was and with a very worried look on his face, he then asked if we knew everything. I just gave him a wry grin and said, "Welcome back home and sorry for delaying you". Poor man was probably and may still be extremely messed up. If you are that man, I do apologise.

The final role we had was 'Towers' or basically manning the guard towers around the prison overlooking the wall. These were remarkably similar to what you see in Second

World War movies on POW camps such as 'The Great Escape' with Spandau MG42's and search lights. We had a searchlight but a different machine gun, the 7.62mm GPMG, the UK's standard medium machine gun. We manned these 24/7 with two men in each of the dozen or so towers around the prison. It was a boring duty, but you had distractions, in that you could see the prisoners in the exercise yards of each H-Block and you could watch the world go by outside, the farmers tilling their fields, our own patrols and the traffic on the M1 motorway. This task however only took half of the troop (16 men of 32 men in the troop). So our Squadron Leader, Richard Shirreff, being an extremely innovative officer dreamed up a concept of supplying a reserve multiple to the Belfast Brigade and in particular the Gordon Highlanders. This partly came about as my 'step' Cousin, Peter Fox-Linton was the Adjutant of the Gordons. The concept was that we sent 16 soldiers led by the Troop Leader or Troop Sergeant divided up into 4 'bricks'. The brick was the basis and smallest part of the patrol make up in Northern Ireland. Four Bricks or more would then form a 'multiple' and a number of 'multiples' would patrol a given area dominating the ground and moving in unpredictable patterns that made attack hard and more importantly, hard to escape from once an attack had been made. This reserve was later expanded to the whole province giving us one-week patrols in places such as South Armagh, Londonderry, East, North and West Belfast, Portadown and other areas. It also gave us the opportunity to work with many other units and organisations that we would not have otherwise done. The Ulster Defence Regiment in East and North Belfast, the Gordons in Belfast and the Cheshire Regiment in Londonderry.

As our deployment came to an end in Northern Ireland it became apparent that we were extremely likely to be mobilised for operations in the Gulf. There was a great deal of speculation in the press about the possibility of a greater commitment by UK to the operation to defend Saudi Arabia and then liberate Kuwait. We handed over to 42

Engineer Plant Squadron RE in September 1990 and set off for some well-earned leave. I headed off to Portugal to visit my sister and her family where I realised that I was suffering from stress as I attacked her one morning when she woke me with a cup of tea. This action was extremely interesting as later I was to discover that the stress of Internal Security operations in Northern Ireland had a far greater impact on me than that of the conventional Gulf War, something over looked nowadays where NI vets are rather forgotten by the Government and the public. I also spent a great week in France with Jerry Denning and Simon Graham, both fellow Troop Leaders from Ireland and good friends. Although we were told we would now be joining 7th Armoured Brigade in the Gulf as part of 1st British Armoured Division. Our promised five weeks leave had been cut to four weeks but we were still not sure of deployment, as it did not seem likely, as 7th Armoured Brigade had literally pillaged our tanks of all components while we were in Ireland.

Chapter 2
Getting Up To Speed.

On returning to York Barracks in Munster from Ireland, we went and saw our squadron tanks in the tank hangers. When we left for Ireland we had ensured that all our tanks were in top condition. We had slaved to make them all A1. In fact the squadron left only three tanks in need of spares and they were on order, otherwise all tanks were operational and gleaming. When I walked into the tank shed I was shocked. Each of the fourteen tanks were standing on their four outer road wheels the central bogies and wheels had been removed. The tracks had been removed, the engines removed, the final drives and front bogey wheels removed, the fire control systems removed, the radios stripped out, the thermal sights removed and in some cases even the crew seats missing. We had become $14^{th}/20^{th}$ Kings Hulk Holding Unit!

The Squadron Leader assured us that new tanks were going to be delivered by the time we returned from leave. However this was not great news, as an experienced Tank Troop Leader I and many others had modified our tanks to make them more operational and comfortable. We had added stowage bins, made adjustments to seats, added codebook holders and other small refinements. These would all be lost as our old tanks had been 'violated' by 7th Armoured Brigade and would disappear with the hulks as they were shipped out. I sent for my troop sergeant and got him to get as many of the lads down to the tank shed that night. We then stripped off what we could save and stored it in the troop store before departing on leave. A worthwhile late night and an effort we were extremely grateful for later.

Returning from leave we were greatly cheered by the sight of new tanks in the tank shed. I used the term 'new' reservedly, that is new to us, as for example the Troop Corporal's tank, call sign 22 (pronounced 'Two-Two', not

'Twenty-Two'), Corporal Ian Simpson's tank was the second oldest Challenger in existence. It had come from the Armoured Research and Development Facility, where it had been used to test modifications for the Challenger II. But at least we had functioning tanks.

We also had three new soldiers in the Regimental jail, all three had been AWOL (Absent without leave) when it had been announced in the Press which Regiments were going to war. One had been absent for a month, the next six months and the final one two and a half years! The first would join us in the Gulf as he was only given 30 days in jail; the other two had to do longer sentences and so missed the 'big show'. I think this shows the great strength of a family Regimental spirit, those three men knew that if they did not return they would be deemed cowards in their community and not able to escape the stigma. I feel great respect for their courage to return but not their initial acts, which were deplorable, however a rare occurrence in our regiment. Not something that can be said for others and I found the behaviour of some abhorrent, particularly a Gunner Bombardier who was hailed by some as a hero for standing up to what he felt was an un-just war and making statements that he did not join the army to fight. In my view I never joined the army to fight but realised that if called upon I was expected to and this is what I swore at my Commissioning. If one wished to enjoy the relatively comfortable life in a peacetime army, you must be prepared to do the needful should the worst happen when political and diplomatic efforts fail. To me this man and the others who deserted were despicable and not worthy of any pity but should be stripped of all that they enjoyed in the soft world of the army during peacetime.

Pre-deployment training started immediately at a tempo that was unbelievable. The efforts made by those who arranged this must be praised and I thank them from the bottom of my heart. The German Army in vast CH53 D helicopters flew us around Germany from one training location to another. These beasts could carry 55 soldiers, so we could fit almost all our squadron tank crews in one airframe. This allowed more time for training as transit to sites was not in trucks and buses.

As a 4th year Lieutenant I was reasonably senior in the Regiment and had covered four training cycles in Germany and done the extremely effective and realistic (as I was to realise later) live fire training in Canada. I had won the Regimental Gunnery Competition in 1989 and taken part in Exercise Iron Hammer, the last divisional Level NATO exercise in Germany in November/December 1988. So I was reasonably confident of my capabilities to lead my troop. However I did have some worries on how I would manage when under fire and seeing tanks destroyed and God forbid if I lost friends. It was a discussion we often had, one such discussion was with my dear friend Jerry Denning. On returning from Ireland where he had been a fellow troop leader of an infantry platoon he was appointed to Recce Troop. The Recce or reconnaissance troop is the eyes and ears of the Battle Group. Equipped with Scorpion Light Armoured Reconnaissance Vehicle (CVR-T) armed with a 76mm cannon and a 7.62mm machine gun and aluminium armour, he felt exposed. I don't blame him, we had 70 tonnes of armour under and over us, and Jerry had 14 tonnes. We also had state of the art thermal imagery; Jerry had Vietnam War era Image Intensifier sights. However, Jerry was an extremely professional soldier and someone I respected and admired, a true professional. It was in the officers mess one night when I vowed to Jerry that if he got into trouble in the desert to our front that I would take my troop to his rescue.

In B Squadron I was probably in one of the best-led and officered units in the Army at the time.
My Squadron Leader was Major Richard Shirreff, educated at Oudle, Oxford and Sandhurst. Richard had been my Squadron Leader in Northern Ireland and I knew him well. He was an extremely professional soldier and the epitome

of ‘leadership’. The soldiers (and Officers) nickname for him was “Well ‘Ard”, as his initials are A.R.D.S.

My Squadron Second in Command was Captain Ian Thomas. Ian had just completed a year seconded to the Regiment as a troop leader from 6th Ghurkha Rifles and was just about to return to 6GR as a substantive Captain. The Regiment therefore requested that he remain for service in the Gulf. ‘Tommo’ or ‘Bahadur’ as all knew him was an experienced officer from 6th Ghurkha Rifles whom the boys had got to know well. Ian was a quiet amusing man who played hard and worked hard, someone us junior officers respected and enjoyed.

Battle Captain, Captain Henry Joynson. (of ‘windup’ fame in Northern Ireland).

Henry Joynson – Battle Captain.

One of Henry’s ancestors had been the last commander of the Camel Corps, and some felt Henry might have stepped into a time warp. Henry was an eccentric entity, something and someone the soldiers loved. He had long experience in B Squadron when the Squadron was based in Berlin and was an extremely fit and able officer.

1st Troop Leader: Sergeant Major Fogg. Sergeant Major Fogg was one of two NCO Tank Troop Leaders in the Regiment and possibly in the whole Brigade or even Division. He was a seasoned soldier with 18 years’ service in a number of theatres including Northern Ireland on four occasions in the 1970's and Germany. His perspective was greatly appreciated by us younger troop leaders and added a huge amount of experience to the leadership pool.

2nd Troop Leader: Lieutenant John Dingley (Dingbat). Four years Troop Leading experience in Canada, Norway, Northern Ireland and Germany with the Blues & Royals and our own Regiment in two full training cycles including exercise Iron Hammer the last full divisional Field Training Exercise (FTX) to be held in the German countryside.

3rd Troop Leader: Lieutenant Johnny Hollands. Johnny was about a year my junior and had become a firm friend. We had served together in B Squadron with the previous Squadron Leader in Canada and on Exercise Iron Hammer. An old boy of Blundells School he had a family military history to live up to. His father having won an MC in Korea.

4th Troop Leader: 2nd Lieutenant Eddie Gimlette followed his brother into the Regiment. Eddie was the junior officer in the squadron and an extremely entertaining man. Eddie was fresh out of Sandhurst and the Troop Leaders' Course at Bovington, so had a very steep learning curve.

Forward Observation Officer (FOO): Captain Derek Hodson, The Rocket Troop, 2nd Field Regiment Royal Artillery. Derek was a great man who had a wonderful sense of humour and was readily accepted into the squadron. He was mounted with his FOO party in the latest version of the Warrior Fighting Vehicle, that had all the latest kit for navigation and targeting artillery and air support, however to fit all the kit in, it had no main armament. The 30mm Rarden Cannon had been replaced with a wooden mock up, it did however retain its 7.62mm chain gun.

left to right: Derek Hodson, Author, Ian Thomas, Johnny Hollands.

Liaison Officer: Lieutenant Hamish de Bretton Gordon 4th Royal Tank Regiment (4RTR).

Hamish de Bretton Gordon, right.

Hamish was seconded along with many support soldiers from 4 RTR and was appointed to the Squadron as our Liaison Officer with the oldest transport in the Squadron and possibly the whole allied force. He was in a 1950's Ferret Scout Car that traced its lineage to the Second World War Dingo armoured car armed with nothing more than his own side arm and a pintle mounted Light Machine Gun (LMG) based on the Bren gun on his open topped armoured car.

Squadron Sergeant Major: WO2 Skip Rae.

SSM "Skip" Rae and RSM Morrow

'Skip' as he was universally known was a mountain of a man who was a former regimental boxer and popular Senior NCO. He also had a Ferret Scout Car as his personal transport that he soon swapped for a soft skinner Land Rover.

The pre-deployment training ensured that we, as tank soldiers were ready for all eventualities. We threw grenades, something many civilians would believe that all soldiers did, however only the officers in the Regiment had done so as it was not thought necessary by the bean counters in the 1980's for tank soldiers to do as part of their training. We also shot our personal weapons, 9mm Browning Pistols and 9mm Sub-Machine Guns (SMG), the modern version of the Second World War Sterling. This was all done at Sennelager, a former Waffen SS training establishment used by NATO to this day. It has extensive ranges for all types of weapons used by the Infantry. We also enjoyed the anti-aircraft range where we were armed with a 7.62 LMG (Light Machine Gun), the modern version of the Second World War Bren Gun mounted on a pole, called a larch pole. We were expected then to shoot down a remote control plane, I don't think anyone managed it and we all hoped that the RAF and USAF would 'dominate' the skies over us, as we basically could not hit a fast jet with machine guns.

We also had extensive time on Biological and Chemical Warfare. This was seen as our major threat and it was interesting to see the change in attitude of my soldiers to this part of training. In the past it was despised by most in normal training, as you got a gob full of CS or tear gas and had to run around on exercise in a hot, uncomfortable and dirty charcoal lined suit. With the threat being very real, we all made sure we concentrated and were able to mask up in time and knew all the indications of chemical attack. Decontamination was also taken very seriously; something in the past which had always been a bit of a joke.

We also got to fire our tanks, a lot! We went on the ranges with our main wartime ammunition, Armoured Piercing Fin-Stabilised Discarding Sabot (APFSDS known as FIN) with a Tungsten 'long' Rod penetrator. This ammunition was capable of penetrating any known armoured vehicle at 1,000 meters. As a result it came with a massive charge to propel it. This was something we had never really fired before. The first time some less experienced crews fired it, they got bruised faces as the kick from it made the 70 tonne Challenger rear up like a startled stallion. On the ranges at Hohne we were amazed at the support we got. Normally range days are hard manual work followed by intense shooting under pressure. The manual part was the need to 'ammo bash' every morning and before every shoot. Tank ammunition comes in robust wooden and metal boxes that are secured with steel banding and seals. All this needs to be removed and then the packaging inside is polystyrene or wood. This has to be replaced in the boxes and placed back onto the pallets for disposal. During the pre-deployment range firing we had soldiers from 2nd and 4th Royal Tank Regiment there to do our 'Ammo Bashing' as well as some extremely depressed soldiers who had been left behind by 7

Brigade. One in particular sticks in my mind, an Australian who was on a year's secondment to the Artillery of 7th Armoured Brigade, but was left behind because the Aussie Government would not let its troops deploy to the Gulf. A Decision that was reversed by the time we were preparing, so the Aussie soldiers in 4th Armoured Brigade came with us.

The actual ranges consisted of some of the most intense training I have experienced. We fired more rounds in the fortnight than we normally fired in two months gunnery camp in normal training. This included firing our smoke dischargers, something most had never done. We concentrated on very long range shooting, something that was to prove vital to our success. We also practiced operating our tanks fully closed down, something that in peacetime training we seldom did for safety reasons. We could also alter ammunition types at our own discretion, a practice restricted in normal peace time gunnery training. This included operating with a full ammunition load that made a huge difference to the space available to us inside the tank. On exercise and gunnery camp in the past, you would stow thermos flasks in the 'ready round rack' (ammunition for immediate use in the turret), beer in the charge bins (storage for the explosive propellant), as they were cooled and maps and the paraphernalia of command in the turret tunnel. All these spaces were now filled with HESH (High Explosive Squash Head), Fin (Fin-Stabilized Discarding Sabot), Smoke (White Phosphorous) and 7.62mm link machine gun ammunition. We did however stow my metal Stanley 2 litre thermos in the ready round rack one day. In a particular intense practice we had a very different sound on one shot but continued to engage targets. This strange sound was not really noticed but it was realised later when after the shoot, we returned to the rest area and decided to have a cup of tea. My loader, Lance Corporal Pomfret or 'Pommers' as he was universally known came up and said he could not find the thermos, so the tea would take a few minutes as he had to brew up using the Boiling Vessel (BV) in the tank. At the end of the day when we had to de-bomb the tank we found that we had one spare HESH Practice round, but no charge for it. It was then quickly realised where the thermos had gone, Pommers had loaded it in the heat of the action. We quietly returned the round to the pile at the back of the range.

Chapter 3
2nd Troop, 'Second to None'

This is probably a good time to introduce my Troop and my own tank crews.

2ND TO NONE TROOP.

SGT MILNER SMITH COWBURN EDDOWS

ZIPPY WOOLSTONHOLM CPL SIMPSON

LEECHY HOPKINS HINDMOOR ME.

I led three Challenger tanks making up Second Troop, B Squadron, 14th/20th Kings Hussars, 'Second to None'. Each tank has a crew of four. A Driver, usually the most junior in the crew, a Gunner, a Loader the second-in-command of the tank and the Commander, the senior soldier in the crew. The Drivers and Gunners are cross-trained and so can either gun or drive and in emergency also load the main 120mm armament.

Two-Zero
Lieutenant John Dingley – Commander
Lance Corporal 'Pommers' Robert Pomfret – Loader, (Replaced by Corporal Lythgoe)
Trooper Andrew 'Smudger' Smith – Gunner
Trooper Paul (Leechy)Leech (Wilson) – Driver

Two-One
Sergeant Donbavand, replaced by Sergeant Milner - Commander
Trooper Jonathon 'Woolly' Woolstonholm – Loader
Trooper, Hindmoor – Gunner
Trooper Richard 'Zippy' Miles – Driver

Two-Two
Corporal Ian 'Simmo' Simpson – Commander
Trooper Cowburn – Loader
Trooper Wayne Hopkins – Gunner
Trooper Eddows – Driver

Inside the Challenger tank the crew lives in very different environments from one another. Which is strange considering how small a space it inhabits.

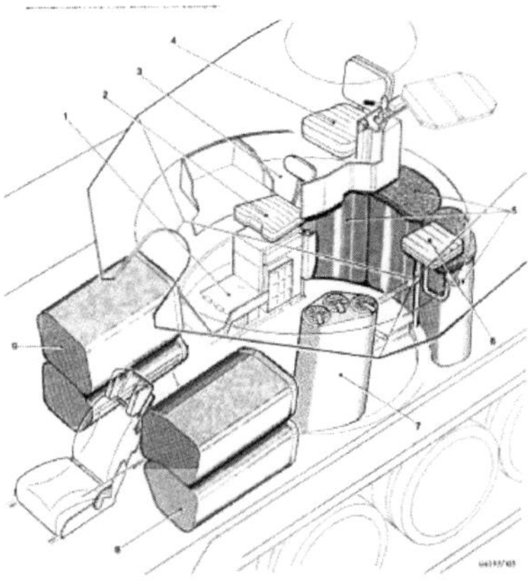

Driver

The driver sits in the hull of the tank closest to the ground at the front. He has the loneliest position as he has no line of sight with the rest of the crew and can only communicate with them through the tank intercom system. However, he does have the most comfortable seat, which doubles most of the time as his bed. He does not sit so much as recline on a kind of 'lounger' and can elevate it to stick his head up out of the hatch on the front of the tank. He controls the tank with two tillers, pull the left and you go left, pull the right and you go right. The tank has four forward gears and three reverse. He has a brake pedal and an accelerator, there is no clutch as the gear box is semi-automatic, with the control on the right side of the cab.

Driver Two One, Trooper "Zippy' Miles.

The brake pedal is positioned centrally and requires a two-footed stamp to stop the tank. Either side of him are extra rounds and charges, and the hull batteries, not perhaps your ideal bed fellows!

Gunner

The Gunner sits on the right hand side of the turret below the commander. His post is extremely cramped and he has no room to stretch his legs. He has no real backrest, other than the commander's knees, as the backrest provided is more often than not broken or missing. To his left is the gun and the spirit level indirect-fire-sighting-system, known as the 'bubble and squeak'. This is an age-old artillery system for sighting a gun and allows the Challenger 120mm gun to fire HESH (High Explosive Squash Head) out to about 22 kilometres. On his right is the range readout, the grip switch that allows him to rotate the turret and elevate/depress the gun and the Thermal Image viewer that looks like a mini TV. He also has a gun-to-hull indicator, a 360 degree direction dial and the emergency manual controls for rotating the turret and elevating/depressing the gun and the reversionary gunnery sight periscope, two things we hope not to need very often. He also has his intercom system. In my tank the gunner, Trooper Smith, had wired in his Walkman player so we could listen to music as we fought our tank.

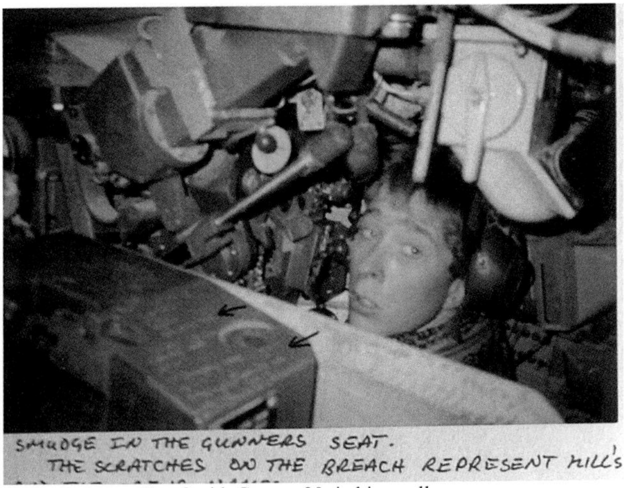
SMUDGE IN THE GUNNERS SEAT.
THE SCRATCHES ON THE BREACH REPRESENT KILL'S
Tpr. Smith Gunner 20, in his small space.

Loader

The Loader is the 'mother' of the crew and he stands, rather than sits, on the left hand side of the turret. He stands a footplate that covers about half of the turret floor with a guardrail that he can rest his bum on while on the move. He is surrounded by ammunition, main tank rounds on the back of the turret wall above the radios, more main rounds on the front turret wall and charge bins around the rear of the turret fixed to the hull floor. Finally 7.62mm link machine gun ammunition in trays at the front of the turret and stowage for our small arms ammunition and grenades.

POMMERS CATCHING A
UNDER THE GUN.
Pommers catching a kip under the breach.

He also has the very important task of manning and maintaining the most important bit of kit in the tank, the Boiling Vessel (BV). This is a square box about 30cm square that can hold about four standard baked bean tins and water. It is used to heat the canned food for the crew and boils water for our tea and coffee. It is a strong belief in the Armoured Corps that if a BV is unserviceable, then the tank is declared 'VOR' (Vehicle off the road)!

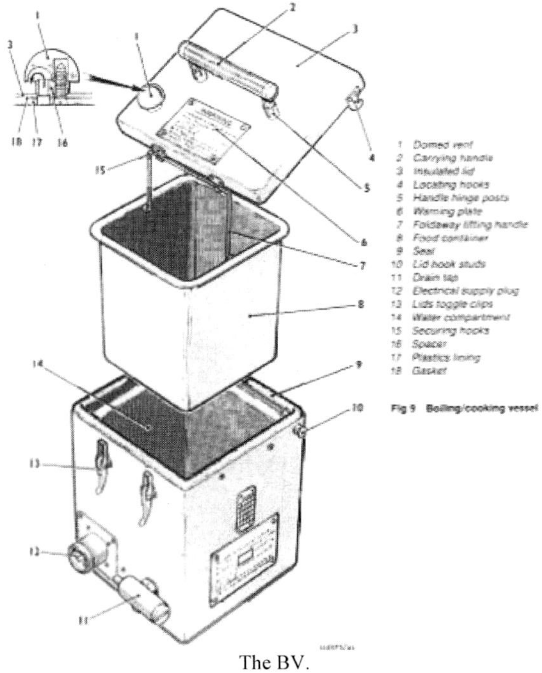

The BV.

The BV has been a feature in all British tanks since 1945. The loader also ensures that the tank has all the ammunition and supplies that are needed and monitors the driver with his tasks of ensuring the fuel and lubricants are in place before moving off on operations.

Commander

The Commander is the senior member of the crew and sits above and behind the gunner on a hydraulic seat that can be raised so he can stick his head out of the turret through the commander's cupola.

Author in the Commanders Hatch.

A double-jointed contortionist was probably responsible for the design of the ergonomics of the Challenger. The controls, sights, switches and fire control computers were not placed logically nor for ease of use. The Commander's position demands the skills of a contortionist break-dancer to operate. The Commander sits with his knees in the back of the gunner with his optical sight in front of him (at just below my eye level so requiring me to adopt a crouched stance). The thumb controller for the turret traverse and gun elevation are positioned to his front right. The elevation and traverse control for his independent commander's sight, linked to the 7.62mm commander's machine gun, are on the upper left of the cupola. This allows the commander to look for other targets to kill while the gunner is engaging the selected target. This is all very well, however having a 1960's gun system, working with a 1970's fire control system, working with a 1980's thermal imagery system contributes to this ergonomic challenge. The thermal sight is mounted to the left of the commander on a bracket attached to the turret roof with the fire control computer on the right of the commander by his hip and the Commanders Range Readout (CRRO) on the roof to the right. This means a lot of left and right, up and down checking on information and data. However the thermal sight or TOGS as it was known was probably the best in the world at that time. We could see a man at over 5kms and a vehicle at over 10 km. It was slaved to the gun with the actual sight on the outside in an armoured barbet or box on the right of the turret.

Pommers and the Author in our "Nomex" Tank suites.
Note the TOGS Barbet on the left in the picture above the smoke dischargers, extra bin on front basket and bedding mats on right of the turret.

Chapter 4
Preparation, the 7 P's
(Prior Planning & Preparation, Prevents, Piss Poor Performance)

We worked hard between training to prepare our tanks for prolonged operations in the desert, a theatre none of us had ever operated in. This included putting the salvaged bins and stowage from our old tanks back on and painting our tanks in desert sand colour. This was done in the hangers of the RSDG barracks in Fallingbostal between range practices. To say it was a hurried job, would be an understatement, we also did not pay too much attention to health and safety, resulting in some rather mind altering paint fume induced highs followed by the most hideous headaches. It was in Fallingbostal that we said goodbye to our tanks as they were then put on flatbeds to Bremmerhaven and shipped from there to Al Jubail in Saudi Arabia. However before we handed them over to the Royal Corps of Transport 'Movers' we sped off to the Fallingbostal NAAFI shop to buy booze. Alistair Todd who had deployed with RSDG had got news back to us that there was no booze available in theatre. The major debate was, would we get mixers in the desert and if so what mixers, as a result I bought a selection of hooch. Johnny Hollands and I decided that the TOGS barbet was a good location to store our stash, as it needs a trained gunner to start up the TOGS and so open the armoured barbet. We discovered that we could fit about four bottles in when opened. That night, Johnny, Eddie Gimlette and myself did a night mission to the tank park and tank by tank started up our TOGS and loaded our illicit cargo. In my case two bottles of Gordon's Gin, a bottle of Famous Grouse whisky and a bottle of Pimms. Sadly when I arrived in the Gulf my tank was not on the same ship as the rest of the Regiment, so I was issued a brand new tank from the force reserve in Saudi Arabia, so some lucky sod got my stash!

Finally with our tanks loaded on ships we concentrated on personal weapon skills, chemical warfare drills, radio message encoding and de-coding, fitness, lots of fitness, turret drills in the gunnery simulator, health and hygiene lectures and enemy and friendly vehicle and aircraft recognition. The enemy vehicle recognition was extremely important to me. I had always been pretty poor at it especially when aircraft were involved, let's face it a fast jet is a fast jet and hard to recognise when passing you at Mach 2. One of the most useful and memorable training days was when we were whisked off by the German army to Soltau in CH53 Choppers to look at 'Bundeswehr Ost' or East German Army vehicles and equipment. We were flown down on a crisp November morning and dropped on the training area. There displayed in the distance was a selection of Soviet equipment including: T72, T62 and T55 tanks, BMP 1 and 2's the Soviet armoured infantry carriers and a ZSU-23-4, which is an anti-aircraft gun system with 4 x 23mm machine guns mounted on a tank or so we thought. There was also a BTR 60, a wheeled armoured infantry carrier and a BRDM, a wheeled reconnaissance vehicle. Lined up on our side of the muddy field were a couple of Challengers from 2 RTR with their gun systems running. We were able to sit in them with our gunners and view the vehicles as they drove past on a circuit. It was amazing how small and hard it was to see the BMPs, they are low and fast, something our own Warrior fighting vehicles were not, we also noted how they resembled our own Spartan APC's. The Soviet tanks were also low profile compared to our Challengers but the T55 and T62 did not have stabilised guns so could not fire on the move. Once the mobile demonstration was over we were able to walk and over climb on, sit in and basically play with all these vehicles.

I made a beeline for the ZSU-23-4, as it was a vehicle we had always been told was a grave threat had the Soviet 3rd Shock Army decided that a trip to the seaside was a good idea. It certainly looked big and imposing, and the four

23mm machine guns looked ‘well sorted’. It also looked compact with its own integrated radar guided fire control system that included a radar dish mounted on the back of the turret. However as I climbed up with Johnny, the turret roof buckled in, in the same way my Golf GTI had done when Jerry had tried to do some urban surfing after a hard night at the Farm Club in Verbier! Basically it was not very heavily armoured at all and we reckoned you could probably brass it up, and certainly make life uncomfortable for the crew with a 7.62mm machine gun, and we had 2 of those on our Challies, let alone a well-placed 120mm HESH. The next surprise was the BTR 60 and the T55 tank. Neither had a bulkhead between the engine compartment and the fighting compartment, so the noise inside the vehicle must have been unbearable. This meant that crew fatigue would be very high for our Iraqi opponents. In all, most of us were not impressed with the Soviet equipment, except for the crew helmets (schlemophon), which certainly made looking in your sights easier and looked really cool but gave little ballistic protection.

It was on the way back from this display that I got a severe rollicking from our Squadron Leader, Richard Shirreff. Stupidly I made or rather started to make the statement; ‘Well I had an Iraqi in my platoon at Sandhurst, and he was meant to be one of their best, and err, well he was crap, in fact useless’, I was then going on to say, ‘So with the kit they have, they should not be too hard to beat’. But was told to shut up at just that moment. It was a sound approach by Richard as it could have led to complacency and that has been the fatal mistake made by many armies. The Yanks in Vietnam, who did not rate the ‘little gooks,’ much the same as the French did at Diem Bien Phu to their cost and the Red Coats at Isandlwana who did not rate the Zulus.

Some of the preparation was extremely good, some bizarre and some just silly. One of the best lectures and presentations was camouflage in the desert given by a

Royal Green Jacket officer. He had been out to the Saudi Desert to visit 7th Armoured Brigade with a team of experts on camouflage. As you can imagine, we were used to hiding in trees and using green camouflage nets to hide our tanks on exercise in Germany. The desert was to prove a very different environment as was later rather amusingly pointed out by an attached Squadron Leader.

The presentation showed us the effect of sun glint on glass, effective use of the ground and camouflage nets in a suitable desert tint of pinkie-brown. When a tank troop was in a dip between the dunes, they could all but disappear in the desert heat and haze from a distance of a kilometre or more. It also allowed a screening of our heat signatures. The glass glint was certainly taken to heart by the Commanding Officer of the Royal Scots, who later ordered the removal of all the windows and windscreens of the battalion's vehicles which made for some very uncomfortable journeys by the soldiers and problems with sand gathering in cabs of the vehicles during sandstorms. Luckily our CO had a different approach, he ensured all vehicles had hessian covers on all windows and windscreens, a simple but effective modification that ensured the vehicles remained comfortable and a haven from sand storms.

One presentation was on STD's or Sexually Transmitted Diseases that turned out to be less important for us front line troops. The presentation was done extremely well by a WO 1 or Senior Sergeant Major of the Royal Army Medical Corps. He had a fantastic squaddie friendly presentation that very quickly had us in stiches of laughter. His opening comments would now be deemed 'non-PC' but they certainly worked. However the opportunities open to us to meet any females and so engage in any 'hanky panky' were to prove extremely unlikely. Not that we knew at that point and I am sure it was probably pertinent to the thousands of REMF's (Rear Echelon Mother F@cker's) in Al Jubail.

In preparation, our Commanding Officer Lt. Col. Mike Vickery told all the officers and NCO's to read the accounts of the Regiment's campaigns in Mesopotamia (Iraq) in both the First and Second World Wars. This was to prove vital to us all. As in one less than helpful presentation on clothing and kit we were told of nothing but heat and dust. As a result many ditched or had plans to ditch their parkas, cold weather sleeping bags and waterproofs. The presentation did warn us about cooler nights and so that jumpers and combat jackets were a good thing to take with us. However the accounts from the Regimental histories talked of bitterly cold weather and rain, yes rain in the desert! As a result most of us kept our army issue sleeping bags that were designed for Germany and worked well as proven on exercise Iron Hammer in December 1989 when we experienced temperatures of minus 15 Degrees Centigrade and snow on the ground. We also packed our waterproofs, in my case my army issue parka. A great bit of kit that had a liner and hood that kept you warm and had big pockets for carrying all my personal kit, so negating the need for my webbing.

Captain Alistair Beverage, the Regimental Officer in command of the A2 Echelon also ordered some very nice sand coloured scarfs or shamags, complete with regimental badge, for use against dust. They were an excellent piece of clothing and I still use mine to this day. My mother also sent me two vital and most cherished items. The first was a suitably light tan woollen Guernsey Sweater. I stitched on the Black Desert Rat insignia of 4th Armoured Brigade on the sleeve and wore it most days. Some other Officers sported their old school cricket jumpers that resulted in a rather colourful mix, including Johnny Holland in his Blundell's First XI sweater and Eddie Gimlette sporting his old school jumper. The second item from Mum was a Palestinian Black and White keffiyah (Yasser Arafat headdress) that she had from my parent's time in Jerusalem in 1960. It was made from extremely fine cotton and stopped the desert dust excellently. I did not at the time realise the significance it must have had on Iraqi's that I met later during the campaign. The final bit of equipment, that I nearly packed in my tank but chose to hand carry was my camouflage umbrella. This I had modified for use above my cupola when on exercise in Germany against rain, something that always seemed to happen when out and about in Germany on your tank, so giving credence to the old army cry, "If it 'aint raining it 'aint training!" Finally, one thing I felt every officer should always have when on campaign was tucked into my kit bag, my shooting stick, which proved to be very useful in orders groups and when generally hanging around or enduring the 'hurry up and wait!' syndrome that the army is so good at in an environment where there is little to sit on other than sand, of which there was a lot.

Finally, we were given our deployment dates. B Squadron was informed we would fly on the 21st December 1990 and so we were allowed a week's leave prior to deployment. I set off to England to see my parents. We celebrated an early Christmas and birthday. It was really the first time I had had time to consider where I was going and what the implications were. I was experiencing mixed feelings, pride to serve my country, excited at being part of the greatest adventure of my life to date, camaraderie with my soldiers who would serve under me and with the Officers I would serve alongside in the greatest challenge of my professional military career. I also felt confident that we, the Regiment and in particular B Squadron would quit ourselves well as we had inspired leadership and 'esprit de corps'. I wondered how we would cope if commanders were lost or taken out in the action. Strangely I was extremely confident that I would come back, this is probably the same feeling that most soldiers have and have had for centuries. My faith was strong and as a committed Christian I relied on my God to guide me and provide me with the fortitude to face the challenges ahead. On my leave I spoke with my father about Faith and took the opportunity to go to church in our village church, St. Peters Draycott.

Prior to visiting Mum and Dad I dropped in on my girlfriend whom I had met while skiing in Verbier the winter before. This was an interesting encounter, as it seemed to be more emotional for me than for her. This surprised me, as I had always thought I was not necessarily the most emotional man. I arrived at her home in London and could only stay a day or so as I wanted to see both my sister and parents before the week was up. Perhaps as she was the daughter of an RAF officer she was used to the 'good bye' moment. I found her very cool and was surprised when she said she could not join me for the trip down to Somerset and West Sussex. It was still a fun two days and we lived it up in London for a couple of nights before I headed off to the countryside.

My visit to Lise, my sister in Haselmere was a far more emotional experience as she was without doubt distraught that her baby brother was off to war. She also had two children, my wonderful niece Natasha Coco and my mischievous nephew Max who was probably too young to understand. However Coco was of an age that she could understand where Uncle John was going and that there was a bad man, 'Badam Hussein' who wanted to kill Uncle John. Coco would cry when Sadam Hussein's face came on TV and would get angry with him, it was extremely sweet to see such a young child have such emotion and understanding about where the threat to her uncle came from. Coco was three years old at the time, and until she was about seven I could scare her up to bed by just saying 'Uncle Badam is coming to get you!' Something that terrified her and I feel guilty for tormenting her with.

I also took the opportunity to buy some personal bits and bobs that I thought would make life more comfortable in the desert and be useful. I visited the jewellers in Wells and bought an Omega watch that had a thermometer, air pressure gauge, stop watch and altimeter, it also had both digital and analogue clocks. This was so I could monitor the temperature and air pressure, two important inputs required in the tank firing system computer. I also bought new cotton underwear, talcum powder, cotton socks and a new camera to supplement my small pocket Pentax. This was a compact 35mm Canon with a telephoto lens that the shop claimed to be robust. These would prove to be invaluable and I bought thirty, 36 exposure, 35mm colour films.

On my return to Germany we had a couple of days to pack and some of us thought about getting personal weapons to augment our 9mm 1911 model Brownings that we called "Nine Millie's". We had heard from friends in the $16^{th}/5^{th}$ Lancers that the German authorities were allowing officers to rush through their Jagdschein or shooting licence so that they could buy shotguns. I have to say we were more thinking of getting hunting rifles rather than shotguns. After all a shotgun is a close range weapon, we already had one of those in our 9mm Brownings and SMGs, what we wanted was something we could shoot long range in the desert. None did get any special weapons, but I had an interesting offer of an Uzi from one of my soldiers who had 'contacts' in the Manchester underworld. We were also issued with our 'Nomex' tank suits, these were special suits only issued in times of war and something none of us had ever seen or used. The initial impression was that they would be quite good, but soon we found that they were pretty useless. They only had a one-way zipper that came to just above your crotch, no access to your trouser pockets, one breast pocket and a map pocket on the thigh with a transparent plastic cover. We took them with us as they were said to be fireproof but few used them, however I did until our cotton desert camouflage uniforms arrived. This was a good example of what not to do with kit or equipment, had we used these suits on exercise we could have advised on their development and improvement to a standard of the German and French tank suits.

We gathered in the mess with the A Squadron officers and Regimental Headquarters officers in the anteroom on the last night for what many of us thought could be the final dinner at the Regiment for some. As we gathered an interesting mood swept through us bachelor officers. However the mood quickly lightened with good banter that continued into dinner. It started to go downhill after dinner when the champagne came out and we drank from 'the sand bag'. This is a solid silver sandbag presented by three former officers to be brought out when someone 'talks shop' at dinner, and we certainly 'talked shop'. The evening then took another 'social abseil' when Henry Joynson informed us all that he was reading a book that he hoped would prepare him for action; by a very good author. He went on to explain that it was a story about a group of German soldiers in WWII and that before they returned to the front they would visit the local brothel. Many of us recognised the story, one we had read in prep school. It was Sven Hassel's series about a group of 'convict soldiers' fighting on the Russian front. Once Henry got over our mirth at calling 'Sven Hassel' a great author it was decided in our drunken state that this concept seemed a great idea. Off we headed with a bottle of champagne in each pocket of our dinner jackets and dropped in on Club 2000. Suffice to say, some had fun, some drank and one met his troop Corporal who was there to collect his girlfriend who worked in the athletic department of the club. We did rib him for a long while about how the conversations would go in the desert between them about this young lady with whom they had had a common experience!

Chapter 5
Deploying to the Big Sandpit

Next morning we woke up at 04.00, drew our personal weapons from the armouries in a subdued mood and gathered outside the NAAFI bar in York Barracks. We were then issued with new NBC suits, combo pens, fuller's earth pads, detection paper for our respirator cases and radiation monitors. These were black faceless watches that we wore on our right wrists to monitor our exposure to radiation. This certainly focused the mind as the combo pens are full of Atropine, a blocker to be administered if you were exposed to nerve agent. The pen would be stabbed into your thigh automatically by the action of shoving it into your leg, there was then a large vallium pill in the cap that you were meant to take to calm you down, not sure it would mind you! There was not much banter and if I remember rightly there were no families. The 'pads' (the army term for married soldiers and officers) had been asked to say their farewells at their quarters. This was a good idea as us single guys had no one to see us off so did not expose us to emotional goodbyes. Not that any of the single officers would have noticed due to the monumental hangovers that we were nursing.

We travelled by coach in the cold December morning to Hanover airport, where we were driven into a vast hanger that had a conveyor belt for luggage leading out to the tarmac. We were then required to pass our kit bags and 'Bergen's' (Army rucksacks) through an x-ray security check, which struck me as slightly incongruous, we were going to war, so when asked by the Royal Military Policemen conducting the checks why I had a knife in my kit bag it made me laugh. I can't remember my response but Pommers had a good one, 'to cut my toe nails!' and that seemed to suffice but I'll use this to kill Iraqis as he unslung his SMG. I then remember seeing a man in an airline Captain's uniform having a heated discussion with a group of officers and so sauntered over having 'Checked in' my kit. The discussion centred on the fact that we were all carrying our personal weapons. Basically he was saying, 'you can't take those in the cabin'. Once again some had not yet made the transition from peacetime regulations and attitude to wartime. Unbelievably, the Royal Corps of Transport movement staff and Military Police were supporting the aircraft Captain. So Alistair Beveridge made a quick trip into Hanover Garrison to 'borrow' weapon rolls for all our personal weapons, including any knives and bayonets that people had on or in their webbing.

Once this fiasco was over we were bussed out in white army busses to the aircraft. This is when we discovered that we were to be flown to war by British Caledonian Airways. An airline usually associated with 'cheap' holiday flights and with a catchy jingle that was soon being sung by us all, 'Wish they could all be Caledonian, wish they all could be Caledonian, wish they all could beeee Caledoniaaaan girls.' As we boarded the Tri-Star aircraft, we realised that there were Caledonian girls on board and they were in great form. All the crew had volunteered for this flight and were extremely proud to be flying the army to war. We settled in to the one class cabin, shoving our webbing and daypacks that made up our 'hand luggage'. Not exactly the normal set size hand baggage and laptop bag one is normally restricted to. Very quickly we were in the air on route to RAF Akrotiri in Cyprus. As we reached cruising altitude I moved to join Corporal 'Simmo' Simpson my troop corporal and Lance Corporal Chris Simpson who had been in my troop in Ireland who were standing in the galley area at the centre of the aircraft. Chris and I had an uncanny resemblance to each other and Simmo shared the Simpson name with Chris and as a result the three of us were known as the 'brothers'. As we chatted up two of the Caledonian girls, Simmo dropped in that we were brothers. Both girls looked shocked and bemused and one asked, 'but if you are brothers, why has he got a posh accent and you guys northern accents?' Simmo, as quick as you like, replied, it is actually a sort of sad story, but John here was the lucky one, you see our parents could only afford to send one of us to a posh school, so he went off to boarding school and we went to the local comprehensive. This immediately got a huge sympathy response for them but not me! So I decided to join Johnny Hollands and Jerry Denning at the front of the plane and discussed how our troops were forming up. Jerry had been very lucky in that as Recce Troop he was the senior troop leader and commanded most of the most experienced crews in the regiment. The importance of information and Recce tasks conducted by Recce Troop were vital to success. Johnny was not new to B Squadron and had a good team under him. My own Troop was moulding into a slick unit, most had served in my troop in Ireland and so we knew each other well.

Being a small Regiment, we tended to know everyone well and had served together in other roles. Simmo had been my Loader in my troop before Ireland and had also been in my troop in Ireland. Leachy, my driver had been in my brick in Ireland and Pommers had been in my brick and also my driver in Ireland. I had also trained many of the younger troopers in Catterick when I was a recruit troop leader after Sandhurst and my tank training course. I also had guys from my troop who had been in Canada with me serving in my two other tanks.

I believed greatly in the British 'family' regimental system based on regional recruiting, the experience of building up a tank troop in a compressed time frame reinforced this. The boys all knew the same places at home, went to the same pubs, supported the same football teams, many creating friendly rivalry and making entertaining nights in the NAAFI bar on 'derby' match nights. I think that this is best demonstrated by the relationship at the very top of the Regiment. As a young 2nd Lieutenant the driver of Lt. Col. Mike Vikery's tank, was Trooper Morrow, now WO1 Morrow the Regimental Sergeant Major, the senior Non Commissioned Officer of the Regiment.

Chapter 6
Landing in the night

My only visit to Cyprus was a three hour stop over while the aircraft was refuelled in the early evening Mediterranean twilight. We were allowed into the RAF waiting lounge and given a brief about our arrival at Dhahran Airbase. We were to have our respirators on our laps and be ready to mask up in the event of a chemical or missile attack on the base.

Airborne again, the mood became a little more sombre, however the Bee – Cal Girls did their best to keep our spirits up. Our approach to Dhahran was at about midnight and we descended steeply hitting the tarmac hard and fast. As we taxied the magnitude of the airlift effort was displayed in stark reality. Under the bright arc lights (no blackout here) were huge American C5 Galaxy aircraft being unloaded at every possible dispersal stand. They carried two Abrams M1 tanks or one Abrams and two Bradley infantry fighting vehicles in their massive bellies. It was surreal to see tanks emerging from an aircraft and to see our Tri-Star dwarfed by these massive airplanes.

As we stepped out of the aircraft door the desert blast hit us charged by the smell of burnt jet fuel and the roar of aircraft of all types. The jumbo jet rumble of C5 Galaxy's and C141 Starlifters, the scream of C130 Hercules and the crisp thundering of fighter aircraft from a number of air forces. British Tornadoes and Jaguars, American and Saudi F15's, F16's and F4 Phantoms. We also saw a line-up of RAF VC10 Tankers, an aircraft I had never actually seen before.

While taking in all these sights, we were briefly distracted as we boarded our buses, the entire crew of the aircraft lined the steps and all the Bee – Cal girls lifted their kilts to give us a sight that would be remembered for a long time!

Little did we know how uncomfortable we would be on our first night in Saudi Arabia. Herded onto a fleet of rather odd-looking double decker buses expecting to go to a terminal and collect baggage. Instead we drove straight out of the airbase onto the highway to the port of Al Jubail. This was a journey of 98 kilometres taken in convoy along a road that was nose to tail with military hardware. Tank Transporters, trucks, Humvees, fuel tankers, cargo trucks, APC's of all types on low-loaders and us in our buses with Pakistani drivers who seemed to have a belief that God would ensure they did not crash into any of these other intimidating road users. This was helped as there seemed to be no traffic going the other way, and in fact the highway had both carriageways dedicated to northbound traffic. It took almost three hours to cover 98 Kilometres and as dawn broke we entered the Oil Terminal area of Al Jubail. We passed camp after camp of green tents stretching as far as the eye could see creating a sea of green canvas between oil refineries and pipelines. One of these seemingly anonymous camps was named 'Black Adder Lines', the British transit camp in Al Jubail. The Royal Engineers had created an accommodation complex in the desert among pipelines and oil facilities that could cater for at least 2,000 soldiers. We were given a tent that 8 – 12 men would share. All the junior officers were billeted in the same tent and we soon got our kit and weapons, which had been ferried up to us in a fleet of 4 Ton Bedford trucks. As soon as we had dumped our kit, we got a hearty breakfast of bacon, eggs, sausages and tomatoes with lashings of army tea. We then crashed out in our pits, this is a good description, as the beds provided were the British Army camp bed, an item that was designed in the 1940's and had not changed since. It is without doubt the worst camp bed in history, as your bum rests on the ground and is so low that you cannot comfortably sit or lay out your kit on it. I resolved myself to get one of the American camp beds that were without doubt the best I had ever seen.

Life quickly settled in to a rhythm of exercise in the morning at 05.30 to beat the heat and blazing sun. We found running in the sand hard work and took pride in overtaking US units who seemed to move at a slow shuffle on the tracks around various tented camps. We also got used to dust and grit that seemed to get into every pocket, bag, pouch, weapon and body crevice. I needed to shower at least twice a day, firstly in the morning, which was uncomfortable as the water was freezing and one found you huffed and puffed your way through your shower. Most showered later in the morning when the sun had taken the chill off the water in the black plastic tanks mounted above the shower cubicles. These cubicles were simple structures with a large black plastic tank mounted on uprights with a watering can rose and stopcock over a wooden shipping pallet. There was a rumour circulating that one unfortunate soldier had been killed earlier in the deployment when the uprights had collapsed and the 10-ton tank of 10,000 litres of water had crushed him, it certainly meant we did not linger in the shower.

General ablutions were pretty basic, with long drops for sitting jobs and desert roses for peeing into. The desert rose is a simple device that is made from a 3 meter length of plastic water pipe buried in the sand with about 60-70 Centimetres sticking out of the ground at an angle of about 50 degrees and a funnel to aim at when peeing. Pee would seep deep into the desert sand and give the flies nothing to attract them.

After a couple of days in Black Adder Lines we were bussed to the port area of Al Jubail to assist in the offloading of equipment from the ships that were coming in at an incredible rate. It was a fantastic feat of logistics to deploy that much equipment and manage to get it to the right place and know what was arriving when. Bearing in mind there was US Marine equipment, US Army, US Air Force, our own equipment, resupply for 7th Armoured Brigade and divisional assets. Initially we were tasked with moving equipment off the dockside and driving all sorts of vehicles to dispersal areas and special workshops set up in hangers on the dockside where desert and hot climate modifications were carried out. We also took the opportunity to do some shopping at the US PX and get Baskin Robins ice cream from the outlet set up on the dock.

It was here that I met my first American Army personnel and was rather shocked at their ignorance. In the queue for ice cream I met a 1st Lieutenant from the Artillery, in fact he was from the Patriot Missile battery on the dockside. We chatted for about half an hour as we queued and as we parted company he said, 'Hey John, it was great to meet you and great to see all you Aussies here.' I was shocked and asked him why he thought we were Aussies, he thought that our Black Rat or Jerboa was a kangaroo! I found it rather surprising that a man of the exact same rank as myself thought there were Aussie ground forces in the Gulf. The only contribution the Aussies made was the few soldiers on secondment to the UK forces and a warship somewhere in the Indian Ocean protecting Diego Garcia. I also took a stroll over to the US Marine camp at the port to get hold of a few of the much sought after US camp beds and a marine floppy hat. I only had my blue beret that cooked your head and green jungle camouflage uniform, our desert camo uniforms had not been issued yet. In the Marine camp I quickly found the stores and with Simmo and Leachy we managed to swap my beret, stable belt and Leachy's combat knife for 6 camp beds and a US Marine 'chocolate chip' desert camo floppy hat. I also took the opportunity to pop into the Marine barber and got a US Marine 'flat-top' haircut. On my way back to our area of the port I bumped into our Adjutant, Captain Johnty Palmer who immediately told me to take off my hat. My heart sank as I realised I had no other headdress now, but he was in fact checking my hair cut having heard that I had been to the US Marine barbers. He said, 'well that's not too bad, put your hat back on and carry on', phew, my US headgear was accepted. I sewed on a cloth 'Shite' Hawk cap badge

and my US Marine floppy was my headgear for the rest of the war. Toby Masterton of the Life Guard Squadron did not fare so well after completely shaving his head. This was deemed to be 'un-officer like' and his Squadron Leader gave him a right royal bollocking.
I distributed the US camp beds to my troop in seniority, so basically all the commanders and loaders got a bed, which certainly was welcomed by all.

It was in this odd period of hanging about for our tanks to arrive that a visit was arranged to The Royal Scots Dragoon Guards in the desert north of Al Jubail where they were supporting the US Marine Corps. It was great to see Al Todd and get some pointers and advice on operating in the desert. Al was rather annoyed that he and his troops could not re-join the Regiment as they still felt a little foreign "penny packeted" out. There was a brief talk of swapping them with one of our Life Guard troops, but as we had trained together it was felt it was better to maintain the existing structure, furthermore the Life Guards were a formed squadron with its full chain of command.

The first thing we noticed was how well equipped and tanned the 7 brigade guys were. They all had desert cams, body armour and all the battle Captains had Warrior fighting vehicles armed with a 30mm Rarden cannon and 7.62mm chain-gun. Our own battle Captain, Henry Joynson had a 1960 vintage 432 APC with a 7.62mm GPMG as his main armament.

On the trip out to 7 Brigade the clutter of hardware in the desert astounded us. In Germany, except for on Exercise Iron Hammer we had never really seen the full Brigade let alone a Division or Corps forming up. Here it was all happening and in a big flat desert. Clumps of camm nets could be seen for miles and yet it seemed that desert real estate was in short supply.

Chapter 7
Christmas Presents

Christmas Eve and Day 1990, proved to be auspicious. It started with the Officers serving the soldiers with 'gunfire' at 6am, a wicked brew of rum, tea and any other alcohol the Quartermaster could get hold of. After a leisurely morning we had Christmas Lunch and again the Officers served the soldiers a full Christmas feast with turkey and Christmas pudding. We then sat down ourselves and had a great lunch, at the end of which we all received a Christmas box from the Royal British Legion which proved a huge hit with all as the contents were extremely well thought through by the British Legion volunteers in UK. The box contained a small black and yellow box torch, lip salve, a small pocket mirror, shaving kit, a hair brush/comb, baby wipes, tissues, cotton buds and some sweets. The most useful Item was the torch. It had two AA batteries that were readily available from the QM stores and was a small box with a swivel head holding the bulb. I later glued the torch onto the back of my commander's sight where it shone on my knees and my map. No light emitted directly in my eyes or out of the turret.

Just after we had finished our Christmas lunch we were told that the Roll-on-roll-off ship with our tanks had arrived. We loaded up on 4 tonne trucks and drove to the port. At the dockside was a huge Danish ship painted white with a massive rear ramp/door that was being lowered as we arrived. The atmosphere was electric and also festive, our real Christmas presents had arrived. Initially the Royal Corps of Transport (RCT) Movers insisted that they were the only ones qualified to off load the vehicles, something we suspected not to be true of the armoured vehicles but probably for the soft skinned Land Rovers and trucks. After all, we were the tank drivers and commanders who drove these vehicles for a living. The process started very slowly but as the soft skin vehicles had to be off loaded first, which was fine but meant that we were somewhat redundant. The Captain, his wife and some of his officers were on the dockside, as they were Danes, I used my best Norwegian on them and this surprised them. I chatted the afternoon away and they shared some Aquavit shots with us. When it was time to off load the tanks and armoured vehicles it became clear the RCT guys were not used to driving Challengers and other armoured vehicles in a confined space. A number were bumped and the final straw was when our Colonel saw a challenger Gun barrel strike the side of the ship. He marched up to the senior RCT man and told him we would off load and there was to be no discussion. We swarmed into the ship 'tout suite' so that there was no time for the RCT to react and started to off load the vehicles of our battle group. The ship was huge with five decks of vehicles where you had to walk over the vehicles as they were parked so closely you could not walk between them. The armoured and tracked vehicles were on the two bottom decks where there was an access ramp from the upper decks about 1/3 of the way from the stern. The ship's crew were great and pleased to have experienced drivers and commanders to help off load as they surveyed the damage to the ships side. Steadily the rumble of armour moving off the ship drowned out all other sounds shattering the peace of early evening as it was about 8pm when the first tank came off and well after midnight when the last emerged. We drove our armoured vehicles and tanks to an assembly area up the far end of the port where the conversion hangers were. This involved transiting through the US Marine Corps camp at the port. The first tank I took with my driver was the 3rd off the ship; as we passed through their camp a number of sleepy Marines gave us a wave, by the time I drove my next tank it seemed that the entire US Marines Expeditionary Force was lining the route cheering and giving their signatory Marine whoop or Uhhharrr, it was a great feeling and made the night entertaining for all. The RCT guys, who were still a bit miffed, started to interfere again and demanded that we go no faster than 5 kilometres an hour, that was 'red rag to a bull'. I off loaded the last tank, it was one of D Squadron's, in fact it was my great friend, Stephen Bryant's Three Zero. I knew that all the drivers and commanders of A and B Squadron were on the dockside and that the rather boorish Sergeant Major of the RCT Movers was at the exit ramp, so I made a rather mad and rash bet with Leachy, I bet him that he could not hit top gear by the time we came off the ship. We had the full length of this huge ship, probably about 200 metres before the rear ramp. Leachy almost won his bet as he hit top gear as we hit the dockside. Johnny Holland told me they could hear the rumble before the tank popped out of the stern of the ship like a champagne cork, later it was reported the RCT Sergeant Major wanted blood, but never found his man. We finally got to bed at about 2am on Boxing Day after a long but memorable Christmas Day.

Boxing day itself was a let-down in comparison with the information that my tank had not been on this ship and that in fact about eight tanks from A and B Squadron would not arrive for a further 2-3 weeks. As a result, when the rest of the Squadron were unpacking their tanks the crews who were tank-less were driven off to the reserve tank storage area. Here were 14 Brand New Challengers with KG registrations and a couple with a KF registration lined up. The tanks we had in Germany generally had a registration with the letters KA in between two numbers. The tanks here had KF and KG registration letters showing that they were far newer. This was a good bit of news bearing in mind we had lost all our extra stowage bins that we had rescued from our original tanks that were stripped while we were in Ireland. It was at this point that my driver Leachy came up with a bit of information, that I can now only admit resulted in a devious move. When I realised the Squadron Sergeant Major was going to allocate the tanks in Squadron and Troop order, I realised I would be left with a KF registration, so I quickly stepped in and gave him the registrations from left to right, not the normal army practice of right to left, this gave me 65KG50 as my steed of war and my good friend Johnny got the KF registered tank.

Skip Ray, our Sergeant Major did comment on my 'non conformity'!

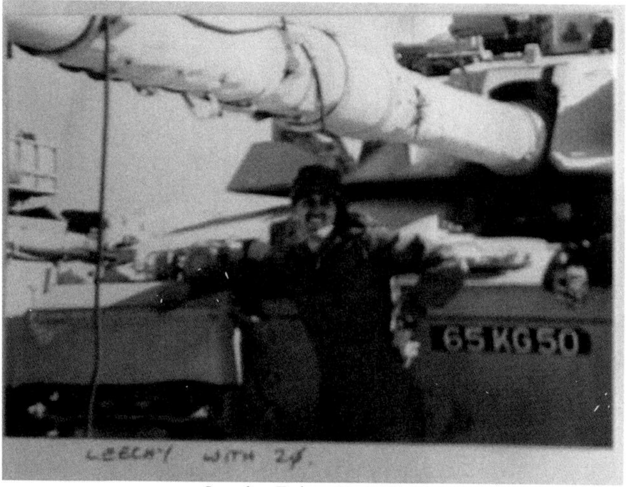

Leechy, Driver Two Zero

Our next task was to go and scrounge as many extra stowage bins as we could. We quickly set out around the reserve vehicle park armed with spanners and managed to 'liberate' a short stowage bin from a 432, a stowage box from a truck and an ammo box, not quite what we had lost but as good as can be expected. We marked up the tank with my call-sign boards, Two Zero (20) and drove our new tank to the Regimental assembly area where we joined my other two Troop tanks, Sergeant Donbavand's Two One and Corporal Simpson's ancient Two Two.

It was some time in these days that we got our first issue of desert camouflage cotton uniforms. We got 2 pairs each and those of us who wanted to, bought Saudi Army desert boots. The new uniforms were a welcome change and the desert boots were comfortable but not very durable and had a rather thin sole that was fine when in your tank but not on sharp stones or uneven ground. We also changed the chemical filters on our tanks and got new spare respirator filters for our personal gas masks as well as a spare set of DPM (camouflage) NBC suits that we were instructed never to open until ordered.

We deployed into the desert on the 28th December 1990 on what was to prove to be the first of 94 days straight living on and from our tanks. We put the tanks on tank transporters on the morning of the 28th at dawn. These were Commander Tank Transporters that were especially designed for Challengers and had the same engine as the Challenger, the CV12 Rolls Royce with 1,200 Horsepower. Our drivers travelled in the Commander Transporters while the rest of the Squadron loaded up onto coaches, one per squadron.

So started our journey to war. As we headed out on the highway I went forward with my tape collection, which is world renowned for being crap, armed with my copy of the 'Sound of Music' I put it on the coach tape deck and cranked up the volume. After the initial hail of abuse the boys settled down and in no time the whole coach was singing along to 'Doe a deer, a female deer, ray a drop of golden sun' along with Julie Andrews … and the other tracks from 'The Sound of Music'. Not the vision one would expect when heading to war. The singing was abruptly cut off when the coach screeched to a halt in a cloud of blue smoke, slightly shocked we looked out for what may have caused this to only see empty desert as far as the eye could see bar the large green road sign that had in large letters, Kuwait 192km's. It then dawned on us, the Pakistani coach driver had suddenly realised we were headed to war and this was how we were getting there, he thought we were going to retake Kuwait in his coach! After about ten minutes we persuaded him that we were in fact turning off the main road soon and joining up with our tanks. A relieved coach driver climbed back in his seat and drove us the final 5km to the RV with the Panzers.

Chapter 8
Training & More Training.

The trip was to a vast area of desert just north of Al Jubail to start training. The first task was to 'bore-sight' our main armament. This was most important for our Thermal sights as they were on the side of the turret and thus quite out of natural line. We also had to ensure the main gun-sight and the reversionary sight were on target. The process involves putting a sight in the end of the barrel of the tank and then moving the gun onto a screen at 1,000m using a central dot in the bore sight. Once 'on' and 'confirmed' by Commander, Loader and Gunner you adjusted the Thermal sight, main sight and reversionary sight aiming points to the same centre point on the target at 1,000m. Finally you locked the adjusters to ensure that the sighting remained accurate. We also prepared our wagons after the move and settled the stowage. Initially we concentrated on Troop tactics and Squadron manoeuvres, we then deployed to the tank ranges named 'Devil Dog – Dragoon Ranges' which had been set up by the US Marine Corps and 7th Armoured Brigade on the coastal marsh. It allowed us to 'bomb up' our tanks for the first time and also test all our weapon systems.

Bombing up was done through a standard battlefield resupply or 'replen'. It involved reaching a specific rendezvous location where you were met by the Squadron Sergeant Major, 'Skip' Rae, who then guided you down a line of 4 or 8-ton trucks lined up but spaced out about every 50 metres. The first stop was the ammo truck for red tipped black L31 HESH (High Explosive Squash Head) rounds and 'Eau de Nile' (watery green) colour with a red band L34 Smoke round or WP (White Phosphorus). These both had the same propellant charges that were half charge size in a cotton cover with a red bottom that had sensitive flash powder. They came as a pair in a black plastic tube with a rip off top. We then moved up to the next truck and loaded Fin rounds (L23 Armour Piercing Fin Stabilized Discarding

Sabot (APFSDS)), these were painted black and extremely sharp so we had four special caps for the rounds stored on the turret ring preventing the loader from skewering himself. The charges for the FIN were the full size of the barrel and orange in colour with a recess for the bottom of the round. Our bomb load was about 64 rounds, depending on what mix we had. In this first bomb load we took on about 40 FIN, 20 HESH and four smoke/WP. We also loaded the vent tubes that came in round brown ammo boxes, these are the flash tubes that are ignited by an electrical charge that in turn sets off the bag charge. The rounds were not boxed as we were used to but came in special hoppers that sat on the back of each truck. This was hard work loading up and took over an hour per tank. Once loaded with ammo we then moved forward to get water and rations. We loaded up with four, four-man ration boxes and filled the internal water tank and our jerry cans. The final trucks were the fuel bowsers. A Challenger could hold up to 1500 litres of diesel in its internal tanks with four entry points. It was preferential to fuel on a down slope to allow the fuel to flow forward and get the maximum load. The fuelling hoses were very large and so a tank could be fully fuelled in about twenty minutes. The final point was the release point, which was usually the Squadron Quartermaster Sergeants Land Rover and he passed up the crew's mail and any other goodies he might have scrounged for us.

We then spent the next few days on the ranges, firing and manoeuvring with artillery support and finally a full assault with the infantry. This was an interesting experience and our first chance to operate with the Queens Company and Number 2 Company of the Grenadier Guards who were our infantry mounted in Warrior fighting vehicles.

Here we certainly got to know our new tank and carried out further modifications with ammo boxes and use of the welding kit on the REME Tiffy's Wagon. The Squadron had a Light Aid Detachment or LAD commanded by a

Staff Sergeant of the REME (Royal Electrical and Mechanical Engineers) 'the Tiffy', Staff Sgt Weir.

Tiffy Wier (REME) and Sgt. Milner.

The LAD had two AFV432's Two Four Alpha and Delta, an ancient Chieftain Armoured Recovery Vehicle Two Four Charlie (ARRV) and a Warrior repair vehicle, Two Four Bravo. These guys were the mechanical wonder boys; "they fixed 'em when we break 'em". The particular modifications we made included moving our own tools under the armoured rear decks from their exposed position on the back deck. We also attached extra bins for storage using HESH round boxes on the front and sides of the turret. It was on the ranges that Two Zero had its first and only mechanical problem, we were motoring to a new squadron night leaguer when we lost all our coolant, a blue puddle formed under the tank and we came to a halt. We soon discovered that we had a leak in our AKTOCS; I have no idea what the acronym means but basically it is an extra set of radiators to cool the gearbox oil. These items date from the history of the Challenger which started life as the Shir 1, a tank designed for Iran before the Islamic Revolution and as such had been designed for the desert. As a result it had these extra radiators that in Germany were never connected. As part of the modifications done to our tanks on arrival in Saudi these had been reconnected, but as many had not been used for years they blew seals left right and centre. Our REME team felt that it was a piece of over engineering so simply disconnected them, put in the Germany bypass and told us to motor on. This quick fix lasted for the rest of our time in our desert campaign. The other major troop mechanical failure also happened in the first weeks of our training. It happened to Two-Two, the second oldest challenger ever built. When we shipped Cpl Simpsons tank, it had a problem identified with its main engine generator drive shaft, it was 'going'. We asked if we should change it in Germany but were told to run it until it broke. So Simo did and so we had to do a complete pack change. This sounds a major task but the REME guys were well trained and practiced at 'pack lifts' and it was done within four hours. However this then contributed to the 'major assemblies' count that the Divisional Headquarters had imposed on 4th Armoured Brigade. There were two lines of thought on managing the supply of major assembly spares for the armoured vehicles in Saudi. The first was to allow a set number to be used for training and then keeping the remainder for the actual war or limiting the amount of mileage that each tank could do based on the number of miles on average that were done with a major assembly breaking. Major assemblies being the engine, the gearbox and final drive. 7 Brigade had a major assembly failure rate of 4.5km, i.e. when the brigade moved every 4.5km a tank or Warrior broke down, this was not very high and something we felt we could certainly improve on and did. Brigadier Hammerbeck, our Brigade Commander argued for the first option, allocate the number of major assemblies that the brigade could use in training and let us train until they were used up. This was a great decision and 4th Armoured Brigade never stopped training and achieved a major assembly failure rate of 100.7km per failure. This was primarily due to the excellent leadership of our Regimental EME, Paul Jaques or Wazz as he was known and the excellent support of our REME LAD's. But probably the decisive factor was the experienced soldiers in the brigade who husbanded their vehicles and took every opportunity to check our vehicles at every halt or pause in movement. One major factor in my view was also that our Regiment, the 14th/20th Kings Hussars had three and a half years' experience on Challenger and B Squadron four and a half as they were seconded to the Blues & Royals. Our two Infantry battalions the Fusiliers and the Royal Scots had three and four years respectively on the Warrior and our Grenadiers had three years. 7 Brigade was made up of the Royal Scots Dragoon Guards who had only been on Challenger for twenty months while the Queens Royal Irish Hussars had just one year and the Infantry, the Staffords had under one year on Warrior.

We carried out simple checks and procedures like banging out our air-filters every day and changing them for new ones on a weekly basis, tightening all the road wheel nuts and checking the idler oil levels at every halt. It was laborious, but certainly it paid off.

The Brigadiers decision meant that over the next few weeks we were constantly mobile and only established squadron hides or leaguers at night. This meant breaking camp every morning and setting up camp before last light or sometimes after dark if we were practicing night actions, which was fairly often.

Night operations on a tank can be fraught with problems, particularly for the infantry around us as our drivers sights were not as good as our thermal gun sights and so they could easily be run over, and we would not even feel a bump or hear the crunch and screams. Once we stopped we would generally go into a troop star with the three tanks reversed up to each other, facing out. Each troop formed four corners of a large square formation with Squadron HQ in the centre. Once formed, we would then camouflage our tanks with camm nets that were a nightmare to erect. The nets caught on everything. We did have a system of flexible poles that slotted into pole holders on the corners to push the nets away from the tank and allowed movement on and off it. However often we would not 'camm up' and would park up in a leaguer. When we did this we were in three lines with the troops forming the outer lines with Squadron HQ in a centre line. The tanks would then point their guns out in all round defence. Two Two as the front right corner tank would point its gun at 45 degrees from front and my tank and Two One put our main guns at 90 degrees over the right side. In the dark this led to quite a number of thuds as commanders, loaders and gunners forgetting where the turret was pointing would step off into a void, where they thought the back deck of the tank was. I did this a couple of times, made worse on one occasion by the fact that I was still wearing my crew commanders helmet and was connected to the radios by the 'curly wurley' cable. This meant that as I stepped off and passed the point that I knew I should have stepped on to the back deck, my head was whipped back by the cable and so I landed flat on my back completely winded and unable to speak or move for about ten minutes. The boys of course found it highly amusing. I did get my own back on Pommers once, when he jumped off the tank over the side but caught his parka on the towrope hook and was left suspended about 2 inches from the ground unable to reach his zip to get the parka off or unhook himself. We left him hanging for about an hour while we had supper!

As we trained we also started to receive new equipment and carryout further modifications to our tanks. We soon had our second issue of desert camouflage uniforms and a second new NBC suit. The army also started to inoculate us against the threat of biological warfare. This started with a series of vaccinations; the first of which we were given was for Myxoma-tosis that did not have any side effects as far as we noticed. However the next batch of injections came when we were given a 48 hour break in training to fit new side armour to our tanks. This was to replace our ¼ inch aluminium bazooka plates with Chobham armour plates over four inches thick. The squadron set up in a leaguer in the desert and stripped off the side plates so we were ready for the new plates. The Regimental Medical Officer, then appeared and we were all lined up for a series of injections in both arms, by the members of the Regimental Band who were also our medics and Regimental Aid Post staff. One of these jabs was for bubonic plague. What then happened was just incredible, within about six hours we started to keel over one-by-one with raging temperatures of 101deg F or more. Trying to work lifting heavy plates and struggling with the massive bolts with a ranging fever in 45 degrees C was probably one of the hardest things I had done physically in the army. We eventually fixed our new side plates which we were told would make our tanks impervious to RPG's which was good, however the whole squadron was down to only a few functioning men. So we spent the next day resting and recovering in what I can only describe as a blur of sweating, aching and feeling like someone was trying to break our bones.

I have to admit that this part of the build-up is a blur of memories, although I have my scrap book and my note books that contained my notes from Orders groups, I did not keep a diary of the exact events as they happened. There were numerous instances and activities that changed our lives in the desert.

Chapter 9
Desert Life and Life's Challenges

A disruptive and potentially damaging event was the removal of my Troop Sergeant, Sergeant Donbavand. He was a crucial member of the team, the glue, an old school soldier and one of the older members of the Sergeants mess, where he had a reputation for hard drinking and playing rough. This unfortunately was the start of his downfall. Prior to our departure to the Gulf, the Officers Mess hosted a Christmas Drinks with the Sergeants Mess and wives as guests, old Donbavand got royally drunk and ended up being a tad rude to some of the Officers and as a result he incurred the wrath of the Adjutant, not a wise move in any situation. To say that the Adjutant had it in for him would be too strong, but best said, he was a marked man. It transpired that while we were in Black adder lines at Al Jubail, Sgt Donbavand had left his dogs tags in the shower and had not reported them missing. In a time of war dog tags are a vital piece of identification and as such are extremely guarded. His failure to report the loss was seen as a major misdemeanour. When challenged about his failure to report them missing he admitted his error. As a result the Adjutant had him removed from my Troop to a support role in the Echelons. It was an extremely sad day for the troop as we lost a vital cog in our machine which had kept the administration of the troop tight. Sgt Milner, who had returned to the Regiment from the Gunnery School at Lulworth where he had been an instructor at the school, replaced Sgt Donbavand. Sgt Milner had been away from the Regiment for a number of years and did not have experience as a troop sergeant, which meant he had a doubly hard hill to climb. Joining a formed troop with strong bonds and learning the ropes as a troop sergeant filling the shoes of one of the longest serving and experienced troop sergeants in the regiment was without doubt a huge challenge. Sgt Milner rose to the challenge and soon settled in. However not without mishap, one of which created one of the best laughs we had had for a while. As he had not been with the regiment prior to deployment he had not read the histories we had been instructed to read by the Colonel and arrived with a very light weight and compact sleeping bag, as a result he froze his nuts off, almost literally and set about getting a proper sleeping bag as soon as he could!

We continued at full tilt with movement training, carrying out all actions fully closed down, something we could rarely do in Germany on exercise for safety reasons. I became proficient at map reading and controlling my troop operating from under armour fully closed down. The squadron drilled on what we called 'Quick Battle Orders', these were a pre-set list of manoeuvres that were numbered to allow a quick movement of the Squadron. For example if the Squadron Leader wanted to do a left flanking attack he would send us the code number 2. This might be encoded or if in contact could be said clear on the radio. The Squadron would then act and the whole unit would move like a fleet of ships at sea, shake out in a pre-set formation and carry out the attack with the front left, front right, reserve troop and intimate support troop designated. The intimate support troop comprise the three tanks that are nominated to work with the infantry and provide them firepower right up to the enemy position and cover them as they then clear the trenches and engage the enemy at close quarters. This was not an enviable task, as a tank's best protection is speed and mobility. As the intimate support troop you roared up to the front line of trenches and then stopped while the infantry 'de-bussed' from their Warriors to engage with the enemy, you then slowly moved forward at walking pace listening to the Infantry Company radio net and laying down supressing fire on targets identified by the infantry and targets we identified ourselves. The dangers of being intimate support troop were also not just from the enemy as the infantry would sometimes hit the back of our tanks with small arms fire, shredding our sleeping bags and kit in the unarmoured bins on the back of the turret. Something that often happened in Canada on live firing exercises, however in the practices we did in the desert, the infantry respected us and kept their aim at the targets and not us, building a better camaraderie.

After about two weeks in the desert we were sent fresh rations, up to this point we had been living on 'compo,' the field rations that had sustained the British Army since the 1960's. Compo is actually very high quality food with such delights as Cadburys Yorkie Bars and steak and kidney pie in a tin, which was a favourite of all. However there were some side effects of eating compo, it being a very high protein and sugary diet with little roughage that resulted in four phenomena. The first was a one-time experience, what we termed the 'Compo block', believed to be caused by the biscuits issued in compo, Biscuits AB, which we thought stood for 'Anal Blockage' but apparently stands for Alternate to Bread. Once you started on compo you found that you ceased to need to go to the loo for about three days, you were then shocked by a short notice twinge, to get on your thunder-box or to go for a 'shovel Recce' at about the three day point. This then resulted in the 'coiler' and 'pastel streak'. Due to the high energy nature of the food that you ate you ended up with a tan coloured deposit that just seemed to keep coming so requiring you to swirl your bum around to 'coil' the 'compo snake'. This process was then finished when, using the best squaddie language, 'your nipper off muscle cut the coil', however as the coil was unbroken and still in contact with your nipper off and the ground, as the top end fell away it brushed your bum cheek leaving a streak, 'the pastel streak' on your bum that needed to be wiped along with the normal places. The final phenomenon was less pleasant but may have been planned as it caused endless amusement to all, that of flatulence, we farted for Britain and as you can imagine in the confines of a tank this could be horrific as well as entertaining. Gunners suffered no end as they sat between the legs of their commanders and many a gunner has got his own back on their commander when he least expected it.

Back now to the fresh rations issued to us, these were meant to give our bodies a break from the constant compo. However it was delivered in a black bin bag to each crew at a replen and we did not get to stop and cook it until the next evening. As a result we feasted on chicken and steak, however that night it began, the groaning and then the urgent zipping sound of a sleeping bag opening in a rush, the rustle of canvas and then the thunder of a man's bowels. This diarrhoea crippled most of us in the troop and certainly I was suffering. It certainly cleaned me out of the compo block but meant that I was on very short notice when I got the twinge. This happened for two days and as we continued to exercise involved some imaginative positions to relieve myself. Quite often this involved me hanging off the side of my tank, still connected to my headset so I could maintain contact with the Squadron and listen to the developing practice battle. On one such occasion I was hanging of the side of the tank, doing my best not to pebble dash the bazooka plates to be disturbed by shouting. I had positioned my tank in a dip below two sand dunes so that I could have some privacy for my squirt, however an entire Syrian Regiment was driving along the top of the dune behind me and cheering. It certainly gave me stage fright and was a far better cure than any amount of Imodium!

We constantly played jokes on each other and it helped with the boredom of desert life where we had no TV, a few books that were treasured and shared, so we made our own entertainment. Leachy my driver would regularly try and catch me out. One of his favourite tricks was to put exhaust grease or boot polish on my commander's sight so I ended up with black rings around my eyes after looking through my sight. I got my own back in my own way. As a child growing up in Malaysia I learned to live with creepy crawlies including scorpions. My childhood friend, Peter Robinson and I used to find scorpions, bate them and then snip off their raised stinger at the end of their tail. This childhood learnt skill I used to 'terrorise' the boys. When I found a scorpion I reached for the nearest first aid kit and took the scissors out to snip off the stinger, I then caught the scorpion in my hands and dropped it in the lap of the poor victim. One of the first victims to this gag was Leachy, I asked Smudger to depress the gun, when the gun is forward over the driver's hatch and depressed it is impossible to get out of the driver's cab. I climbed up on the front of the tank and dropped a particularly large sand coloured scorpion into Leachy's lap. The scream was heard in the SHQ over 200 meters away and bought the Squadron Medic, Lance Corporal Walker running. Like Houdini, Leachy had managed to get out of his cab in about 5 seconds, around a 5 ton gun barrel. It was a while before he played another trick on me.

Another favourite was the 'phantom turd' game. This was a favourite in Germany, but far harder to achieve in the desert. It involved sneaking up behind someone who was taking a dump, sliding a shovel under his bum, catching their 'Compo coil' and moving away with it. I am afraid, it does not matter how many people deny it, everyone looks at the result of a shovel recce or dump. The shock on someone's face is hilarious as they search desperately for what they know they have just produced. Checking of overalls, trousers and shirts for the errant turd.

We also had to conduct the most mundane of tasks such as washing our clothes and bathing. Both certainly did not live up to the glamor of being a Hussar getting ready for war! No batmen for officers in this war, I generally made a washing bowl out of plastic sheet in a hole in the sand and hand washed my clothes then hanging them out to dry on the camnets.

Author doing his dhobi.

There were no secrets in a tank troop and crew as you lived in such close confines. Even ones attempts at keeping clean and having a good strip wash were public events, generally involving trying to keep your feet in a canvas bucket while soaping up and rinsing off in cold water. We sometimes would put a jerry can on the back decks to warm it through from the heat of the engine to make things a little more bearable and reduce shrinkage!

Sgt. Donbavand having a desert bath.

One slightly upsetting event was getting a 'Dear John letter'. This arrived soon after we deployed into the desert and although at the back of my mind I thought it might happen, it still came as a shock. Most of the single guys were getting girlfriends and pen pals, me nah, I was dumped. It amazed me that a woman could be so callous, sending a Dear John when a man is heading to war, in my view not a very patriotic move. This however then left me free to get some pen pals that were writing by the thousand to the special post box for such letters, BFPO 3000. We would get all sorts of letters, some with graphic and erotic photos from desperate women, some from sweet old ladies, some from school kids and whole classes sending their best wishes and small gifts. It was much appreciated to know that we were cared for and also helped us spend the few idle hours we had each day. In fact at one stage Richard Shirreff lamented at the time of the Russian peace effort, "well if they negotiate a peaceful solution to this war all I will be able to claim I did was eat compo and write 'bluey's'", this was the name given to the blue aerogrammes that we were issued and could be sent to and from us for free.

My soldiers helped me over my 'Dear John' by leaking to the Star Newspaper that their Troop Leader had been dumped and needed a pen pal. I never saw the article but got a letter from a young girl who said she had heard about my situation and so I started a pen pal relationship with her. She was 21 and worked for the Royal Mail. We also had fun replying to some of the more lewd letters including one addressed to a pilot. It started with 'I want to climb into your COCKpit and feel your thrust', this was just the start and it got far more unprintable. The subalterns and Squadron 2IC Ian Thomas gathered in Henry Joynson's battle waggon, named Baghdad 1917, commemorating one of the Regiments battle honours to formulate a suitable reply. Initially we apologised that we were not pilots but tank commanders, who had 120mm pieces, a big turret and we did have 'long-rod penetrators' and a 'joystick' to control our elevation etc. I don't think we ever got a reply, or if we did Henry kept it to himself!

We soon got the clearest indication that war was imminent when we were issued with our NAPS pills (Nerve Agent Pre-Set). These pills are designed to give you an extra five seconds to react when suffering a nerve agent attack so allowing you time to stab yourself with your combo pen. NAPS had a varied reaction on us all, I personally, once on NAPS lost all sexual urges and had no amorous thoughts at all. Others however wandered around with a constant 'towel rail'... I believe my experience was in the majority which was a good thing for the gunners of our tanks! One wonders what the long term effects may be?

On the 17th January the air campaign started. It just happened that the 18th was the first day we had had off and were preparing to do our personal administration, laundry and sorting ourselves out after twenty one days living in the desert on our tanks, moving almost every day. The incessant beeping of a chemical alarm going off woke us in a panic, the nerve agent detector or NAIAD had alarmed, we masked up and dived under underneath our tanks or into them. This soon proved to be a false alarm, but was closely followed by a second alarm; this was then followed by a third, fourth and fifth all before 8am. At this point I thought enough was enough, I was obviously not going to get my kit sorted so put on my respirator and crawled under my tank and lay down. I was soon sound sleep and slept the sleep of a man who was exhausted. So you could say I slept through the start of my war, not the glorified or heroic start I had imagined. However I learnt a lesson, as when I was eventually woken up by Pommers for lunch I sat up and cracked my head on the hard steel of the hull the whole troop found this extremely funny. Actually it hurt like hell and for a couple of days I Sported a small 'egg' on my forehead.

During all this activity and training we had numerous visits from generals, politicians and the new Prime Minister, John Major. This day was memorable for a number of reasons. Firstly, we were informed at the last moment to move to a set location in the desert as an un-named VIP was coming to talk to us. We had been in the middle of a battle group attack and so the Squadrons were very spaced out. As we moved it soon became apparent that the Life Guard Squadron attached to us commanded by Major Jamie Hewitt had driven into some 'sabkha' or quick sand. This had been the bane of training in the low-lying coastal areas of Saudi. Sabkha is a crust of hard sand that forms on the top of a glue like grey mud that seems to be bottomless. It can often hold the weight of a tank but if the tank turns or slows down it cracks and sucks you in. As we formed up, we could see the entire Life Guards Squadron in a hull down position with the entire battle groups CRAV's trying to recover them. It soon became apparent that this would take hours if not days, so we all had to mount up again and move a kilometre or so west to ensure that our Prime Minister and the accompanying press did not get to see this massive debacle. Some say it was a great ploy by the Commanding Officer to direct them through the area so we as a Regiment could enjoy the 'lime light'.

The Prime Minister duly arrived on the Brigadier's tank and was greeted by the waiting Press pack and us. It was at this point that we knew the war was definitely on, Kate Aide was there. Our Regimental 2IC, Godfrey Tilney monopolised her time rather and I was kept well away from all as I had once again incurred the wrath of the Adjutant.

In the officers' mess opposite my room in Munster was a pair of pictures of Officers of the Regiment in the Desert from the 1st and 2nd World Wars. The Great War picture, had the officer dressed in a tropical tan uniform wearing a pith helmet and the '39-'45 war officer was dressed in much the same desert tan but wearing his red side hat, sometimes likened to a ladies 'bits'... cap . I felt that as we were off to the desert I would live up to this picture and, given the opportunity, donned my bright red side hat. I had after all seen the QRIH wearing their Green 'Tent' hats which were very similar and an equivalent order of dress. So I decided that this was a good opportunity to honour my predecessors. Apparently as we walked down the 800 metres to the area where we were to meet the PM I stuck out like a sore thumb and the question was asked 'who is the Pratt in a red hat?' 'Dingley' came the reply, Johnty Palmer, the Adjutant let me know his mind and told me to take it off and stay in the back ground, so went my effort at a bit of panache and cavalry spirit. My gunner Trooper Smith, an accomplished artist, loved it and so did a pastel sketch of me in my red hat, in my hatch with the pad and pastels my parents had sent to him.

Author, (Photo by Ian Simmo Simpson)

To our surprise we experienced torrential rain. All of us firmly believed that the desert is usually a rather dry place, and so my umbrella came into its own. On one particularly long Brigade move we were convoying as a squadron packet and it was literally running in rivers down the frontal armour. In such rain all the other tanks closed down so as not to get wet, but I had my umbrella up and so remained opened up with fresh air blowing in my face; allowing the crew to enjoy the cool air as a closed up tank in wet conditions creates is a horribly humid damp place. As we motored along I saw a Japanese 4x4 come racing by in the opposite direction, as they passed my tank I saw a face I recognised from ITN and he obviously visualised a great shot of us coming down this track; with only one tank commander visible and sporting an umbrella no less!

The wet road to concentration area Ray and near fame.

The vehicle turned around and drove at break neck speed to pass our column and the camera crew all jumped out to set up the camera. At this our lead tank, commanded by Sgt Bailey opened up and the hatches flopped back like a line of dominos falling; so ruining my moment of fame, or so I thought. It so happened that Robert Fox from the Daily Telegraph had written about my umbrella in the paper on the 1st February, something I was unaware of until much later when my parents and many friends wrote to say they had read about my umbrella.

General Sir Peter De La Billiere, the overall UK Commander in the region, visited us as did the Divisional Commander, Major General Rupert Smith. General De La Billiere was an experienced desert warrior having served with the SAS in Oman during the Dhohar campaign and worked in a number of appointments in the Gulf States. On the occasion of this visit I seemed to be the only one with a camera and clicked of a photo that I know takes pride of place in my Squadron Leader's home. It is of The General with our CO and Richard Shirreff beside his tank 'Bucephalus'.

Left to right: Gen De la Billiere, Lt. Col. Vickery & Major Shirreff beside Becephalus, Zero Bravo.

I am not sure when or why the decision was made to name our tanks but it was. In Germany, we had never named our tanks as some regiments did, but the word came down that the regiment should do so. As we were B Squadron, we were told to use names starting with the letter B. Richard being an Oxford graduate and rather more intellectual than most of us chose the extremely fitting name of 'Becephalus', Alexander the Great's horse. During this process of choosing names I fortuitously received a letter addressed to 'Troop Leader', 2nd Troop, B Sqn, 14/20H,

BFPO 16. It was from a former Troop Sergeant of 2nd Troop, B Squadron, Bob Wood who had fought in the Korean War with B Squadron. In his letter Bob told me that they had not lost a tank in his entire time in Korea and that the troop's tanks names were: Belvoir (pronounced Beaver), Bellman, Beeswing and Benny (in those days they had 4 tank troops). I had no choice but to name the tanks thus as it felt to me like a good omen and provided some historical links to the past glories of the Regiment. This 14/20H Troop in Korea was attached to the 8th Kings Irish Hussars under the leadership of Lt Ted Paul who had won a draw in the mess between three officers to command the troop. Included in the package was a South Korean Flag. We were also ordered to put the Black Rat or Jerboa on our tanks identifying us as 4th Armoured Brigade, Smudge used his artistic talent to make our own Black Rat have a heavy machine gun with the logo below 'Rip Shit'.

Author with Belvoir's Black Rat.

So 2nd Troop, B Sqn 14/20H in the Gulf War rode on, Belvoir, Bellman and Beeswing. We kept the name Benny in case we got a Dozer blade for any of our tanks. As it was

Cpl Adesile of 4th Troop was issued with probably one of the best bits of equipment received up to that point, the dozer blade. The previous Chieftain dozer blade had been an abject failure, it was under powered, caused break downs, lost its hydraulic fluid and was a pain to use as it took about twenty scrapes of the soil to create any sort of worthwhile hole and berm to hide a tank in. The Challenger dozer blade was unbelievable. With practice Cpl Adesile could create an effective tank position in three to four minutes with two to three scrapes.

42 - CPL ADESILE
"THE NIGGER WITH THE
DIGGER"
Call-sign Mike Four Two preparing our berm.
(Note the camnet poles for raising the camnets over the tank.)

I had worked with Cpl Adesile or 'Doughie' as he was known in my first posting with the Regiment in Catterick, he was a 'man of colour' and great character, always playing tricks on people. One such trick caused me great embarrassment. It was at the time of the Guardsman Stokes affair and racism was becoming a major problem for the

Army to address. On the first morning of a new recruit troop Doughie came up to me and asked if I could do a South African accent as I gave the troop the morning orders, I duly obliged to then notice a big grinning set of teeth in a very black face, that of Trooper Williams, the first black man to join the armoured corps for a number of years and he was a 14/20 Kings Hussar. This was particularly worrying as only two weeks before I had been summoned to the Colonel's office and briefed by him about the new recruit and I was to ensure there was no repeat of the Guardsman Stokes affair (a case of racism) in the Armoured Corps. The troop staff and particularly Doughie thought it hilarious. Luckily Trooper Williams also saw the funny side. Doughie soon adopted the 'Nom de Guerre 'The Nigger with the Digger!' Something today which would be not tolerated.

We also added some personal additions to our tankie 'crew guard' helmets and put our names on them. A 'Nom de Guerre' appeared on the back of mine, 'Dingbat', a name Jerry Denning had always called me, so I wonder where that came from. We also put '2nd to None' on the front of our helmets. Mine had a helmet cover on as well so it was less likely to reflect sunlight.

In another incident during the work up training, I had probably the most challenging discipline experiences in my army career to date. We were in a Squadron leaguer after a hard day's training and servicing our wagons and getting on with the mundane tasks of personal administration. I was on the back decks of Two Zero helping Leachy check the oils and filters when the young trooper on stag (guard) wandered up. I said hi and we had an exchange of jibes, which was innocent enough until he pointed his loaded SMG at me in jest. This is a serious violation of all military discipline and both Leachy and I shouted at him to put his weapon down. I then gave him the biggest bollocking I have ever done in my career. He knew how wrong he had been and so I left it at that and did not charge him, he became an excellent soldier and served the rest of his career in the army.

Our own weapons were probably the most dangerous things at this point in general. This we found one morning as we prepared for the day's training. We were in a tank hide with the three tanks parked in a star with the back decks almost touching facing out enjoying the first rays of the dawn sun burning off the morning chill and drying off the dew. Woolly was cleaning his SMG on top of Two One with Sgt Milner doing his teeth on the back decks. I was standing on the back deck of Two Zero packing away kit in the large stowage bin on the back of the turret with Leachy when there was a report of a gun and a 'zing' as a round went between us. We both looked at each other and then heard Woolly scream, 'shit I am hit,' Sgt Milner had also had a close escape as the round had passed by his ear, but immediately started first aid on Woolly who had been shot in the knee.

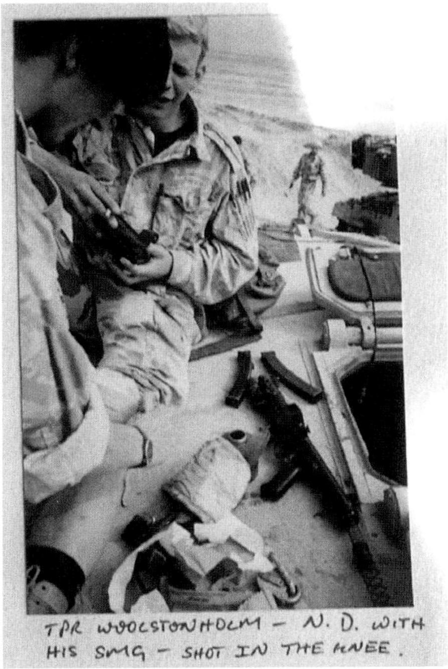

TPR WOOLSTONHOLM - N. D. WITH
HIS SMG - SHOT IN THE KNEE.

Pvt. Tait treating Tpr. Woolstonholm

We called the Medics, Private Tate and Lance Corporal Walker who also acted as our Squadron Trumpeter and they raced over with the Sqn Ambulance, a 432 APC with stretchers and all the first line medical equipment. Woolly was quickly stabilized and shipped off to the Regimental Aid Post and then on to the Field Dressing station and further back to the Field Hospital. It was a real time practice for the medical chain, that worked well, which gave us some added confidence if we ever got hit. Once Woolly was on his way, we carried out an investigation into what had happened. It turned out that he was not shot directly but had fragments of 9mm bullet in his knee from a ricochet. He had been cleaning his SMG and after cleaning was testing the working parts that require a magazine to be fitted as the breech block locks back. His error had been to fit a loaded magazine and not use the empty one he had, which was on the top of the turret with his cleaning kit. There was a blue grey chip in the turret paint that showed where the bullet had hit the turret roof and broken up sending fragments into Woolly's knee and the main bullet past Sgt Milners head and between Leachy and me. The story did not end there. We assumed we would not see Woolly for the rest of the War and started to prepare for a replacement Loader in Two One. We did not get one and continued to operate with a 3-man crew in Two One for a fortnight, when out of the blue, Woolly hobbled up to the troop. He had in fact only three small fragments in his knee, which had been removed and dressed. As he could walk reasonably well within a few days he persuaded the doctors at the Field Hospital that he was fine and bluffed his way through every argument they presented. Firstly they said he needed his dressing to be changed every day, he said, "I am a full combat medic and can do it myself with the Sqn Medic", not quite true, but it worked. The next was that he would need physiotherapy, he responded, "I am a trained PTI" (Physical training Instructor) and could do his own physio! What a bluffer, but it worked, as he checked himself out of hospital and hitched lifts up to the Regiment from the rear area.

The Regiment also managed to uphold Regimental tradition and hosted a dinner for the officers of the Battle Group including the commanders of the attached units, such as the Queen's Company, No. 2 Company Grenadier Guards and the Rocket troop of 2nd Field Regiment Royal Artillery. The dinner included the Loyal Toast and toasts to the Regimental Colonel in Chief, the Princess Royal and finally a toast to the 'The King of Sweden' given as a tribute by the Rocket Troop, of which he was the Honorary Colonel. Unfortunately due to the short supply of booze and seats at the table, the subalterns of the Regiment were not invited. We did manage to get hold of some alcohol free beer called Swan Lager. We drank a case on the back decks of my tank, Johnny, Eddy Gimlette and myself. We chatted about what we thought it would be like, how our boys were shaping up and if the photo taken earlier that day of all the Battle Group officers outside the Regimental Headquarters Tent complex would become the ‘red X’ photo in the mess of those who did not make it. It was interesting the effect of drinking the beer, we sort of felt we were getting drunk but knew we were not, but it certainly helped us pass the night. However the real kicker was in the morning, when we all woke up with hangovers complete with a headache from hell and all without actually getting drunk!

The Red X Photo?

Soon after this event we started a major move to the west to position us for the ‘big right hook’ that General Schwarzkopf had planned for the assault on the Iraqi lines. This started with loading our tanks onto the Commander Tank Transporters again and then the crews being flown by helicopters to an RV with our panzers. It seemed strange to be flown by the navy in their Seaking helicopter over the sands of Arabia. The smell of jet fuel and the dust storm as we took off and later landed were certainly something memorable. The crew was great and assured us that flying over the desert and navigating over it were much like being at sea, both ultimately are featureless. This was a mixed blessing as they delivered us to the RV on time but without our kit, also our tanks had not arrived. This did not bode well as our tanks were our homes and we had little with us other than our personal weapons, webbing kit, NBC Suits and water. So it seemed that an uncomfortable night was in prospect. Luckily our tanks arrived late that night and we off loaded them in the dark and slept on the back decks.

Author with Henry Joynson, Ian Thomas (Sqn 2IC)
With Simmo larking about in the back ground waiting for the Panzers to arrive.

Chapter 10
Deception and Positioning

The next morning we started a major exercise that took the whole of the British 1st Armoured Division westward in part of a great deception plan. It had been calculated that the Iraqis would assume that the main point of attack would include the British Division. As we manoeuvred we practiced all numbers of actions and re-practiced and re-practiced. It was during this move that we also experienced yet more rain. The rain fell overnight in a light shower that cooled the ground which gave off an earthy smell much like I had experienced in Malaysia after a dry spell. The air cleared and the desert seemed to spring to life. In no more than twelve hours the whole desert had a covering of fine green grass as far as the eye could see, it was an amazing sight.

By the time we took up our final location we were an extremely slick unit. This new harbour area was not far from the Iraqi border and so we were put into troop berms. This was a ten-foot high sand wall with one entrance and exit that we covered with a dismounted GPMG in a bunker that we constructed with an old pallet for the floor and a roof covered with two layers of sand bags. We also built another bunker on the outer wall covering the NE to NW quadrant of the Squadron position with a second dismounted GPMG, some grenades and binoculars. All four troops were arranged in a large square with SHQ in the centre in its own berm. My efforts to fortify our position were met with some ribbing by the other troop leaders and Johnny Hollands christened 2nd Troop berm, 'Fort Laramy' after the Wild West fort on TV.

Tpr. Cowburn on 'stag' at Fort Laramy Sentry post

The days here were in general boring and rather mundane as we were stationary and pinned to our hides. This led to some lethargy and poor discipline during the morning and evening 'stand too'. In my troop this manifested itself with some poor noise discipline over a couple of days that was heard by SHQ and in particular Richard Shirreff. After failing to curb it, I was summoned to receive a dressing down, or as Sergeant Major Rae put it, "Sir, get your arse over to SHQ for a severe listening too"! I was quite rightly given a huge bollocking and as punishment for not dealing with the incident, I was ordered to carry a HESH round with me where ever I went. It was a novel punishment and certainly worked, as having to explain to all and sundry why I was carrying the HESH round was most embarrassing. We certainly had the best noise discipline of any troop after that. Once again we had rain and so our patch of desert was again covered in thin grass that made it look rather wonderful and reminded us of the Canadian prairies. It was probably this grass that attracted our first prisoner to our area. It was the day before the 'Khafji' attack in the east that took place on the coast road from Kuwait to Al Jubail. We had been put on full alert and so ‘stood too’ in our bunkers and tanks. At about 02.00hrs we saw movement to our front and Troopers Cowburn and Hindmoor in the bunker called out the challenge, I ordered Leachy to start the tank and we got the thermal sight up and running to look at the enemy, what we saw was surreal, it was a donkey. I sent out ‘Zippy’ Miles and Eddows to bring in the rather sad looking fellow who was happy for some water and green compo beans. We tethered him to one of the tanks and I attempted to report our first prisoner, whom we dubbed Lt. Abdul. I think SHQ thought I had flipped and am sure Richard was wondering how to replace the delusionary officer in 2nd Troop. Next morning to show our captive off and in contravention of the Geneva Convention we sent Leachy over to SHQ with him carrying our water jerry cans for refilling. We kept Lt. Abdul for about two weeks and he carried our water every day, however his love of compo beans outstripped our supply so we decided to let him escape.

Leechy leading The POW working party

The weather was also extremely important to us, in particular the prevailing wind direction. As the Iraqis had started to fire the Kuwaiti oil fields so when the wind came from the NE the sky darkened and we were covered in a black haze that left a dirty sooty residue on all exposed surfaces and on us.

Being static for so long also brought some other problems, particularly with hygiene. Up to now we had just taken our dumps in the desert and moved on. Now we had the whole Squadron in a single area surrounded by the other Squadrons and regiments. We designated areas for relieving one's self. These were in full view of everyone so one's habits and timings became common knowledge.

Communal crapper.

Richard Shirreff was the most regular man we ever saw, after stand too, he headed off with his book or latest bluey from his wife and OMD80 thunder-box and like a clockwork soldier dumped away.

It also became quite social as we sat on our thunder-boxes and chatted. The preferred thunder-box was an oilcan that contained the OMD80 engine oil. Green, round with a capacity of 20 litres we cut out the bottom and the inner part of the top. Some put padding on it and a carrying handle. It was thus quite comfortable and usually stowed with a bungee on the back of the tank.

From this new location we could see the effects of the B52 strikes on the Iraqis and also the effect of 'Daisy Cutters' on them. This was a campaign waged by the USAF to demoralise the Iraqis to our front. Apparently the Americans still had a large stock of these fuel air bombs from the Vietnam War where they were used to clear helicopter-landing sites in the jungle. When these went off we could feel the concussion, and we were miles away; lord only knows how the Iraqis felt. The Americans were doing a lot of psychological warfare that they termed Psy-ops. Once one Iraqi formation had been 'given' the daisy cutter treatment the neighbouring units had leaflets dropped on them saying 'did you see what happened last night to 32 Brigade? … well you are next, see you tonight!'. The Psy-ops guys also came and recorded the sounds of our Challengers driving around, working through the gears. This was then later played to the Iraqis on the front line on the Kuwaiti border to spook them and trick them into thinking we were well to the east. This deception plan also meant that we were on strict radio silence so that the Iraqis could not direction-find the location of the UK Division. This radio silence meant we were not able to move or continue training with our tanks. We did however carry out personal skills training and TEWT's, Tactical Exercise Without Troops. This involved some officer study days where a given Squadron Leader presented one of the basic acts of battle/war. The first TEWT of the day, which will always stay with me, was conducted by the Life Guard Squadron Leader, Jamie Hewitt. His presentation was on the frontal attack, possibly the simplest manoeuvre in war, and he started like this; 'Err OK, so today I am going to cover the attack and err well as you may have noticed this place is not like Germany. Err there are no trees or hills to hide behind, errr or Gasthaus for orders groups so err, let me hand over to my 2IC who will cover the presentation.' This was greeted by some barely stifled giggles and laughs! The other Squadron Leaders then covered the flanking attack, withdrawal and counterstroke battle in a professional and detailed manner.

During this period as we had a lot of time on our hands I decided to send the films I had from my two cameras that I carried at all times to my parents in UK for processing. I also got the addresses of all the next of kin of my entire troop and sent them to my father. I identified each next of kin with a call sign and instructed him to send the photo of the crew taken in Al Jabail that I had taken on the day we deployed to the desert. This was greatly appreciated by all the parents of my soldiers. However poor Mrs Milner ended up with a photo of Sgt Donbavand, poor lady, as he is no oil painting!

CREW 22
TPRS, EDDOWS, COWBURN, HOPKINS, CPL SIMPSON
Photo of the crew of Two Two sent by my Father to their next of Kin.

Sgt Milner had not joined us when the picture was taken, something she mentioned in her thank you letter. This proved to be a great morale boosting event both in the desert but also at home. My parents received some very kind letters from my soldiers' families, most, of which have pride of place in my scrapbook and are reproduced at the end of this book.

However, as can only be expected tensions sometimes built up in the close confines of the troop and within the individual tank crews. One such clash of personalities had been brewing in my tank between my loader, Pommers and my gunner, Smudger. This had really come to a head during our final manoeuvres when we were all very tired after constant movement and tempers were frayed. As we sat in a fire position taking a break from the movement Pommers and Leachy were taking a kip as Smudger and I covered our arcs of observation. Suddenly Smudger saw something and so traversed the turret, unfortunately he did not shout a warning as was normal he simply moved the 18-ton turret. Pommers who was resting on the turret ring with his clip on seat was thrown to the floor and the loaders seat crushed in the one inch steel loader's guardrail which was now bent into an 's' shape. Pommers leapt off the turret floor nursing a bruised shoulder, leaned over the breech and punched Smudger. In reaction Smudger reached for his 9mm Browning Pistol and started to draw it, I rammed him into his gun sight and held him there with my feet. I ordered him to stand down and ordered Pommers to apologise. Pommers begrudgingly did and I also got Smudger to explain why he had not followed basic drills and given the cautionary order 'traversing'. He had no real explanation. Once we stopped for the night, I had a word with both men and felt the matter was over. Unfortunately it was not, Smudger went to see 'Skip Rae' the Squadron Sergeant Major and accused Pommers of bullying him. This was reported to Richard Shirreff who then without consulting me made, in my view, a terrible judgment call. The first I knew of this was when I was called over to SHQ and informed that Pommers was going to be moved to First Troop under Sergeant Major Fogg and be the loader of One Two and I was to get One Two's loader, Corporal Lythgoe. I was in shock and protested, asking why. When it was explained I cried foul and informed Richard that he was moving the wrong man, after all it was Smudger who had tried to draw his weapon, I could not justify Pommers hitting Smudger, but the whole situation was just wrong. I went back to 'Fort Laramy' in shock and called Pommers over, as I told him I saw one of my toughest and best soldiers break down and cry. Pommers and I had been together for over four years, I had fought for his first stripe, and again when he lost it after a scrap in the NAAFI bar. He had been my driver and 'oppo' in Ireland, he was more than one of my soldiers, he was my friend. Unfortunately my protests fell on deaf ears and so the exchange took place that afternoon. I have to say, with Pommers gone there was a big hole in my tank and in the troop, but Cpl Lythgoe, 'Lythcat' whom I had worked with in my previous tank troop before Ireland and he had been in my platoon in Ireland fabulously filled this void. He became one of the best loaders I ever had and was actually a far better cook than Pommers!

We quickly got down to moulding as a team and battle prepping our tanks. This included some new armour for our tanks, a smoke generator for Two One and changing the tracks on Two Two. Track changes in perfect conditions are a full troop task and take the best part of a day. Two Two's tracks were slack and had reached the end of their life. Normally in Germany on exercise you would need to tighten the tracks of a tank about once a week, however in the desert this was reduced to about once a month. The tracks also shone bright silver, as they were sand blasted as they rotated. On the day before the track change the tracks were delivered in four pallets and placed outside the troop berm. The next morning after stand too at 5am we started to lay them out and moved Two Two out of the berm. This was hard graft made harder by the uneven terrain we were working on. However we soon managed to complete the track change before the sun set. Two Two was ready and we had a lot of old track links. As my troop had not received its ERA, Explosive Reactive Armour for the exposed front glacis plate we devised a rig to hang three lines of five links on the front valance of each tank.

TPR SMITH + ME.
IMPROVISED FRONTAL ARMOUR – SPARE TRACK LINKS.

Improvised frontal Armour on Two Zero.
Note the short 432 stowage bin on the side of the turret.
(Picture from RAC Bovington Tank Museum)

We also hung four links from the rear spare link racks on the rear of our tanks for added protection. We thought it looked quite cool and Leachy even made them look cooler by reversing the links so the spuds on the links stuck outwards, very 'Mad Max' looking. A couple of days later I heard that the Regimental Headquarters (RHQ) had a spare ERA set as they were delivered in sets of three and there were only two tanks in RHQ, the Colonel's and the Second in Command's tank. I rushed over to RHQ as I was informed that they were in the process of burying the spare ERA. We buried a lot of kit that we had no use for in the desert, which will make for some interesting archaeological thesis in a century or two. I found the ERA by a large hole and asked the RHQ Troop to hold on the burying operation and headed to the first Land Rover I could see. Here began one of those farcical 'wild goose chases' that only the army can create. This Land Rover was the Regimental 2IC's, Major Godfrey Tilney. I was told to get his permission to use the vehicle to move the kit. So I delved deep into the

RHQ Tent and Sultan Command Vehicle complex and found him in the regimental alternate Command set up. I explained I wanted to borrow his Land Rover to move some kit that was going to be buried, he then said I should get permission from the Regimental Quarter Master Technical, Major Brian Drayner. This was fine but he was at the A2 Echelon, positioned about 5 km's away and Godfrey would not lend me his Land Rover to go over there. I then saw a passing REME Warrior ARV and flagged it down and got a lift over to A2 Echelon. Here I found Brian and he then told me that I should check if I could have the kit with the EME, Captain 'Waz' Jaques, who was based at RHQ! So once again I set off, luckily bumping into Sgt Donbavand who grabbed a Landy and took me back to RHQ. I found 'Waz' and at last had someone who had his head screwed on. He was amazed at my tale and said I could borrow his wagon to move the kit. We de-cammed his wagon and set off to the hole, loaded the ERA up and bumped over to my troop location, Fort Laramy. Here we took the links off Cpl Simpson's Two Two and with a few modifications fitted his tank with the ERA. Now we only had two tanks lacking ERA in the whole Regiment, Two Zero and Two One. We got the ERA for two Zero and Two One a week before G-Day.

Two One's smoke generator was a 'Heath-Robinson' affair designed by Lee Fuller and a couple of Craftsmen at RARDE on the fly. It was a base tank lift pump fitted in a dummy jerry can with a pipe leading from one of the fifty-five gallon drums to the right hand exhaust port. It was activated by flicking on the convoy light switch. These drums had been an addition added in Al Jubail to provide us an emergency supply of fuel.

E.R.A. - RECIEVED 1 WEEK BEFOR
G - DAY.
ERA Fitted to Two Zero.

Maintenance in the desert was very different in general and extremely affected by the weather. In Germany, rust seemed to form on our guns, in the barrels and on the obturator rings (The breech seals) in a day or so. In the desert rust only formed the day after rain, which meant we only needed to clean and oil the guns after rain. We tried to keep the oil down to a minimum as it attracted sand and dust, which actually created more wear on the parts covered in oil. In general spare parts, when needed, came through quickly and were carried in the A1 or A2 Echelon however not everything was available.

Barrel Cleaning, Trps Hopkins and Hindmoor with the push rods.

One item that we missed sorely was the bearings for my tanks NBC (Nuclear Biological Chemical) fans. These fans forced air through two air filters in the back of the turret so that the tank could be filled with clean air forming an over pressure inside the tank which keeps any chemicals out. The bearings had worn out from over use about three weeks before as we manoeuvred west. Our tanks were not air-conditioned as many may think. So the only ways to get the air moving in the hot turret, where temperatures regularly reached over 100 Degrees F, was to either open the commander's hatch and have the engine take its air through the turret or, if closed down, run the NBC system blowing air from the vents at each crew position. This meant that we were faced with going into a fight with an enemy who had chemical weapons, had used chemical weapons and we felt was highly likely to use them on us with no collective protection beyond our own personal respirators. It seemed that life might get pretty nasty for us in Two Zero if Sadam used chemical weapons. Not a good feeling! We managed to get hold of a CAM handheld chemical detector that looked like a futuristic laser gun, but was in fact an air sampler. Our plan was to have this in the turret and for 'Lythcat' to monitor it.

Chapter 11

Orders for War

As we prepared we were briefed on the complex operation that was to be called Desert Storm. This involved being shown a sand table model of the Iraqi defences that the US 1st Infantry Division, The Big Red One, would breach on G-Day and from which we would then breakout.

This was a chance to meet mates from other regiments and the guys of 7 Brigade whom we had not seen since we visited them outside Al Jubail. This led to a stark realisation; there were huge discrepancies of kit between 7 Brigade and us. All troops in 7 Brigade had body armour. It was after this meeting that we coined the name 'The Four-gotten Brigade' for ourselves and they were known as the 'Brigade of Plenty'. In the 'Four-gotten' Brigade it was only the Infantry and drivers of soft skinned vehicles who got body armour. They all also had three sets of desert camouflage uniforms and desert boots, we had Saudi Army boots that we bought with our own money through the QM. They also had far better vehicles for their battle Captains. Henry, our Battle Captain did some up armouring of his 432 by welding old bazooka plates onto the sides of his wagon with a gap of about 12 inches that he then filled with sand bags.

Henry Joynson on Zero Delta, 'Baghdad'.
Note the sand bags and extra armour.

He also took some of Two Two's old track links and put them on the front of his vehicle adding a few tons to his veteran vehicle.

The next training was to see a full scale model of the Iraqi defences that we were allowed to view and walk over, we then did a full drive through of the whole operation in the back of a convoy of 4 Ton trucks, one per Squadron with all tank Commanders on board. This was interesting but also incredibly tedious as we rumbled down Lane Kilo through the mocked up defensive berm and minefields to our release point at Report Line New Jersey. The D Squadron 4 Tonner with the 2IC, Captain Nick Orr, Captain James Cheshire the Battle Captain, and Troop Leaders, Stephen Bryant – 1st Troop, Andrew (Rick) Harman – 2nd Troop, Sebastian Pollington from 2 RTR – 3rd Troop, Charlie Mowat – 4th Troop, the Sqn LO John Moore from 4 RTR and Jerry Denning, the Recce Troop Leader were pulled over by a very irate Royal Army Medical Corps Lieutenant Colonel as they were mucking around, kipping and generally showing little interest in the whole exercise. In the words of Stephen Bryant, "I did not see there was much benefit in driving down a road with Big Red letter K's lit up with cylumes (Glow sticks), a good kip was far more important." We did this twice and did a full rehearsal in our tanks at night as it was anticipated we would move through in the dark. It was during this exercise that I lost a dear friend.

I was standing on the back of my tank when the Adjutant, Johnty Palmer drove up to me and climbed up to join me on the back decks with a sombre look on his face. He told me he had some bad news, Ed Whitehead of the 16th/5th Lancers had been killed when his CVRT Scimitar had overturned that night and he had been crushed unable to get down into the turret in time. Ed was a tall man whom I had got to know well when we both represented our regiments at skiing and we shared a chalet in Verbier for two seasons. I don't know why, but I assume it must have been shock, but I said to Johnty, "no that can't be right, Ed is not here, Ed is in Germany". I mixed him up with an old school friend who had gone through Sandhurst with me, Guy Whitehead, who was a 5th Enniskillen Dragoon Guard and was in Germany. Johnty must have been confused at my denial and left me to ponder. It did not take me long to realise I had lost a friend. My troop left me to my own devices and I sat on my own for a long time praying and trying to remember Ed's smiling face and his outrageous downhill skiing suit, which was a borrowed cross country skiing all-in-one. I think the realisation hit me at this moment that I should find my peace with God and so I sought out the regimental padre, Captain Michael Weymes. He was a Catholic Father, but in the army was expected to be multi-domination and covered all faiths. I asked him if he could confirm me as a member of the Church of England. I had never done the confirmation course at school when most my contemporises had and as such felt lacking. My faith had always been strong and my upbringing had been very Christian, with Church every Sunday at home in Malaysia and School Chapel at Uppingham. My father was a lay preacher at our village church in England, my mother active in the church and my sister working as a missionary nurse, so I knew what I wanted and what I felt God wanted.

I had some long chats with the Padre over the coming weeks and he corresponded with my father on the subject, then in a small quiet ceremony I was confirmed and took my first communion at the Regimental Church Parade. I had attended all the Church Parades from the moment we arrived and it was interesting watching the numbers increase the longer we were in the desert and the closer war loomed. At my first one, I think there were about twenty officers and men and at the final one a few days before G-Day, I think the whole Regiment was present less those on guard or radio stag.

Final Church Parade.

As the air war progressed and we listened to the BBC on the SHQ short wave HF radio and as various peace initiatives came and went we realised that we were going to definitely be committed to battle. I would wander over to 3rd Troop to chat with Johnny Hollands or over to D Sqn where my dear friend Stephen Bryant commanded 1st Troop. We would sit out after stand down at dusk and watch the flashes of the artillery raids that our gunners carried out as well as the B52 bombing strikes hitting the Iraqi front lines and discuss what we thought it might be like; how we would feel if anyone was knocked out. It was interesting, as we showed no bravado as one might expect, in the words of Robert Fox, we were far more philosophical and reserved than the Paras that he had been imbedded with during the Falklands war. Boredom and killing time was in some ways the greatest challenge. Mail calls and a delivery of newspapers helped and became a highlight. Even answering BFPO 3000 letters became a relief.

CATCHING UP ON THE COURT AND SOCIAL
Reading the papers in Fort Laramy.
Note the bunker behind for local defence.

Finally we were ordered to SHQ for the orders of a lifetime, 'Orders for War'. Richard Shirreff presented these orders as any others, with clear instructions on the ground, order of march, weather and the 'actions on', which were to be based on what the Americans were facing as they secured the breach in the Iraqi defences. Basically, if they were facing heavy armoured forces 7 Brigade would lead as they were 'armour heavy', if it was infantry, then 4 Brigade would be first as we were infantry heavy, but in both scenarios 14/20th would lead 4 Brigade with A Squadron followed by B, then the Life Guard Squadron and finally D down Lane Kilo of the breach system.

I returned to my Troop to give troop orders, bidding my friends, Johnny and Eddie Gimlette God speed, I think Eddie said something like, 'well this is it', or something completely un-profound, which rather reflected the mood at that moment.

ME GIVING THE FINAL 'O' GROUP FOR WAR !!
LEECHY. SIMMO. SGT. MILNER ME.

Giving Orders, trying to be serious was hard with Sgt. Milner & Simmo acting up!

I think this was because we had been training so hard for this moment; it came as less of a shock or surprise. What did come as a shock was the notice to move rapidly being reduced to three hours and in about twenty minutes to one hour. This all happened 24 hours earlier than the orders had indicated. In the initial orders we were expected to move the tanks forward the final 40km's on the tank transporters to preserve them, but as the US 1st Infantry Division Mech, 'The Big Red One' had met lighter than expected resistance and were reaching their objectives, 1st UK Division was rushed forward. We rapidly de-cammed our tanks and loaded up the final bits and bobs before motoring on our tracks to join the longest and heaviest traffic flow of tanks, APC's, Aardvark mine clearance flails, trucks, self-propelled guns, ambulances, engineer bridge-layers, fuel trucks, ammo tenders and Land Rovers I have ever seen, with wheels on the right and tracks on the left.

We soon reached the final staging area under low cloud that scudded across the sky. We were lined up nose-to-tail in unit columns that rather worried us as we thought we would be 'stonked' by Iraqi artillery, but it never came. Normally you would have a spacing of about 100m between vehicles but this had been reduced to about 50m. We were told to get some food on and rest if we could, well I certainly could not rest. We could hear the fighting to our front and realised it would not be long until we were in the fight. After only an hour or so we were called forward by the Royal Military Police who were managing traffic control through the breach in cooperation with their US counterparts.

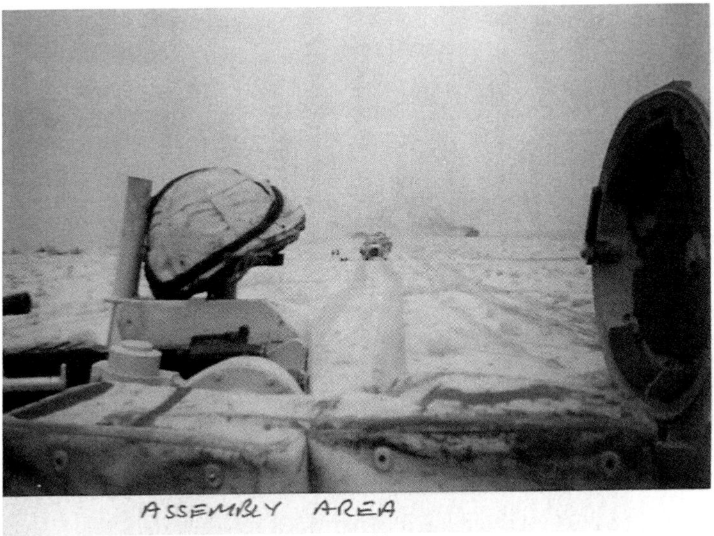

Lining up at the Assembly area.

We soon motored up to the breach itself and passed through a number of checkpoints and the massive red-letter boards with a white K on them guarded by US MP's in Humvees.

Chapter 12
Charging into Iraq

Our way to Iraq and war was along Lane Kilo, one of many cleared through the Iraqi defences by the US and UK Engineers.

US MP's guiding us through the breach.

We stuck to the tracks as these had been swept of mines and any deviation could lead you into a potential killing ground of anti-tank mines, which the Iraqis had laid in their hundreds of thousands. The low cloud made for an apocalyptic scene with dusk falling quickly as we moved forward to our start line, phase line 'New Jersey', the furthest exploitation of the Big Red One. Just as we reached the release point of the breach itself, I had one of those extraordinary encounters that if you were writing fiction you could not make up such a tale. At the release point was a Royal Military Police Lance Corporal standing beside a Bombardier Motorbike with an SMG and a clipboard. We happened to halt for a moment and he signalled that he wanted to talk to me, so I waved him up onto my tank, he crouched beside me on the turret and seemed very dejected. He explained that his job was to 'tick off' each unit as it passed on his prepared list. I took a quick look and saw that all units were there but none ticked. So I told him all 7 Brigade had gone through and this was now 4 Brigade and ticked of A Squadron and B, telling him Life Guards were next and then D Squadron. I said once he saw lots of Warriors that was the Infantry. As we were talking there was fighting going on no more than a few hundred meters away and a T55 was burning to our front. He kept ducking as explosions occurred; I then felt real pity for a Military Policeman for the first time in my life. What a 'pants' place to be, less than a kilometre from the fighting with no body armour, armed with a 9mm SMG and mounted on a motorbike, tasked to record each unit, and no one was stopping to tell him who they were. It was at this point he asked the most mind blowing question, "have you got any spare 9mm ammo sir?" I said, "You what?! You got to be kidding me, how much have you got?" He said, "20 rounds." At this point I just could not believe my ears, he did not even have a full magazine! So I yelled above the sound of battle to Lythcat to grab two 50 round boxes of 9mm and gave him two hand-grenades as well. He nearly kissed me!

We then moved through the carnage of the 'break in battle' with Iraqi T62 and T55 tanks burning and American Abrams tanks and Bradley fighting vehicles securing the front line. It was here that I saw my old chum Jerry Denning who was marking the route up to our start line with the CVRT's of Recce Troop.

Jerry Denning marking the Start Line.

He shouted up a greeting and told me of the first vehicle kill in the regiment. Cpl Wiffin's Scorpion had been run over by Lt. 'Rick' Harman's Challenger and had been crushed in the fading light but luckily no one was injured. As we formed up I heard on the radio that One Zero, Sgt Major Fogg's tank had hit the rear of the tank in front with its barrel bending it and damaging the gun recoil system. Sgt major Fogg had changed tanks with One Two, This meant that my old loader, Pommers, spent the war with the REME forward base workshop trying to get it fixed and missed all the fighting. It did however became the most photographed tank of the war as most the war correspondents stayed with the rear echelons and so it was used by Kate Aide et al. as the back drop for many a report.

Chapter 13
First Contact

At about midnight we formed up on our start line and moved forward in the set formation we had practiced over and over again, 3rd Troop front left, 2nd Troop front right with the squadron leader between us and slightly back. Behind us 1st Troop was rear left and 4th Troop rear right with Ian Thomas, the Sqn 2IC between them. Behind him came the SHQ packet, with Capt. Henry Joynson being driven in his 432 APC by Cpl 'Johnno', Johnson. He led the Sqn Ambulance, the LO in his Ferret Scout car and the two LAD CARRV's as well as the Tiffy's Warrior ARRV.

Our first objective was 'Objective Bronze', all objectives being named after metals. As we advanced into the night with 7 Brigade on our Left I became the right-hand troop of the right-hand battle group. Fairly quickly I saw contacts ahead on my thermal sight. I could make out six BTR 60's with large antennae on the top meaning they were command vehicles, BTR 60 PB's. I called in the contact and was told to hold fire as it was feared it might have been our own Recce or an artillery forward observer unit. The caution was due to the fact there was a great concern about 'blue on blue' contacts in the confusion of the passage of lines with the Big Red One (1st Infantry Div. Mech.).

Richard Shirreff then ordered 4th Troop to make a right flanking probe. As they moved they were engaged by the enemy. As the contact was light armoured vehicles I asked Cpl Simpson in Two Two to engage as he was loaded with HESH and Sgt Milner and I had FIN loaded as we were on the flank. This is a standard practice as our main threat was other tanks trying to attack us in the right flank. Simmo being central was protected by us on the right and 3rd Troop on his left from such a flanking attack so was loaded with HESH for just this sort of eventuality. HESH is much better suited to destroying a BTR 60 as the FIN would just punch straight through the vehicle. That is when our carefully laid plan started to follow the truism, "No plan survives contact with the enemy". Simmo reported he could not see the target! So I told him to "watch my trace" on the radio, which meant to watch where my 7.62 GPMG tracer rounds went. We fired two bursts from the coaxial machinegun and he still reported not seeing the target, so I said "fuck it, Smudger, FIN Tank On! Load HESH" the correct fire order, and change of ammunition type, just the expletive was not quite drill. Our first round hit with a small burst of sparks, we fired our second round, the newly loaded HESH at the next BTR 60 that exploded with a far more satisfying explosive flash and burst into flames.

Simmo immediately reported he could see the target and engaged himself. Literally the moment after he fired we got the urgent cry over the radio to "check fire, check fire, friendly vehicles to your front". It seemed like an age but was actually less than a minute or two at most that we got the signal to re-engage, as it was not friendly units. This pause was the longest of my life. I felt as if someone had kicked me in the balls; I had a metallic taste in my mouth, I felt sick and it felt as if there was a hole in my stomach. I almost lost my ability to function and it was only with huge effort that I was able to get a grip of the situation. Later in the war there were blue on blues by US aircraft, I cannot imagine how they managed to continue to fly their aircraft when informed of the blue on blue. I was almost unable to operate my tank, let alone fly a plane. As we re-engaged, Sgt Milner moved up on my right and we began to destroy the remaining BTR 60's with HESH. I then got a message from Henry Joynson in Zero Delta, the Battle Captains call sign, "Two Zero, you are being illuminated by IR (Infra-Red), I can see it in my II sight". IR was used on many Soviet Tanks and the T55 and T62 of the Iraqi Army were equipped with IR searchlights for night fighting. Leachy confirmed that his image intensifier (II) driver's sight was being blinded which was a sure indication that we were in someone's sights, but as we scanned around with the thermal sight we could see no source. There then occurred another one of those 'fog of war' experiences. There was a massive bang! As I had my hatch open slightly to keep the air moving due to our lack of NBC fans I got a knock from the shock wave on my helmet, dust came in through the one inch gap in the hatch and my thermal sight washed-out. Smudger and I were at the time laying on to shoot at the next BTR 60 but the tank lurched back in reverse and very quickly we were rocketing back across the desert in high reverse. I shouted at Leachy, "hey, what the hell are you playing at? We are trying to shoot up here!" He replied, "Foock off sir that nearly hit us," I then responded, "don't be stupid that was Two Two firing." We were still rocketing backwards-swerving left to right, when he said, "Foock off sir, Two Two is two hundred metres to our left!" He was absolutely right, I had been so in the zone, that when I experienced the bang, knock and thermal sight wash-out I thought it was Two Two from peace time training experience. In training on the ranges in Germany the tanks were lined up on the firing point with no more than a foot between each tank, so when the neighbouring tank fired, its muzzle blast created the exact same situation as I had just experienced. Once I realised, which was very quickly, I saw through my thermal sight a large hot crater merging with our left track mark on the desert sand and watched with horror as the next enemy round exploded directly between the hot track marks we had left in the desert sand exactly where we had been seconds before, Leachy had saved our lives. I reported the contact and ordered Sgt Milner to move, but as he moved he was also engaged and lost his gyros and 'metadynes; in his turret control, so was not able to continue the fight and I saw him heading back across the desert with his turret spinning. I then tried to call Simmo in Two Two, but got no response. Fearing the worst I concentrated on trying to locate what it was that was shooting at us. We scanned the desert and all we could see was one hot spot, and when I say spot, I mean a dot on the thermal sight. The spot then ballooned into a big flash and I realised what it was, an artillery field piece. We were looking right into its barrel at about 500m.

There was a massive explosion to our left as we moved and we engaged with HESH. It was very hard to see the gun as it was behind a sand berm with only the muzzle pointing over it. The battle then settled into a bit of a game of cat and mouse, as we engaged with HESH and machine gun but in their protected position it was hard to get a hit. I soon noticed that before they fired two to three heads would poke up above the berm and duck down if we fired our coaxial machine gun and then pop up again when the rounds stopped. So I set an ambush, using my commander's machine gun. Utilizing the thermal sight to range it so the fall of shot was on the berm I ordered Smudger to fire a burst and five seconds after he stopped firing I fired a burst from the commander's machine gun, the heads popped up right into my burst.

The Iraqi gun crew continued to engage us but less accurately and we then identified two other guns in close proximity to the first. By this time, Simmo was engaging, but I still did not have good communications with him but he was 'on the job.' This engagement, was quickly using up our supply of twenty HESH and they seemed to have no effect on the target gun positions, so I ordered Lythcat to load Smoke and we put four smoke rounds on the position. This then silenced them and we moved up to the BTR 60 position. As we approached we could see Iraqis emerging from their trenches with their hands up. We started to go through the position when six Iraqi's with their hands up blocked us by kneeling right in front of us.

Leachy tried to move the tank right and they shuffled right, left and they shuffled left. As this was going on they were shouting, 'George Bush, Margret Thatcher,' Leachy then opened up his hatch and got his SMG out and shouted at them to move, threatening them with his gun. This just made them all the more keen to cheer George Bush and Margret Thatcher, so Leachy asked me on the intercom, "can I shoot them Sir, they have the wrong Prime minister?" I laughed and told him this was not a shooting offence, popped my hatch and climbed out. I told Lythcat to cover me with his SMG, drew my 9mm pistol and jumped down to the prisoners. I grabbed the first one by the scruff of his neck and dragged him round the side of the tank motioning him to lie down on the ground beside the tank, his mates followed very quickly. As I was doing this, Lythcat noticed that one of them threw something and shouted down to me, so I jumped into the cover of the tank, but nothing went bang. Just as I was dealing with the last prisoner the Colonels Tank 'The Emperor', roared up and off jumped Captain Johnty Palmer, who as the Adjutant served as the Colonel's loader. He flamboyantly cocked his pistol and grabbed the nearest Iraqi, shoved the pistol in his ear and shouted at him, "Where are your officers?" It was then that I realised that I had not cocked my own pistol! So had a ridiculous thought, and pulled the hammer back on the pistol so 'it looked loaded', not really appreciating that it was dark, drizzling and there was no way that these Iraqi's would notice where the hammer was. Johnty did not get much out of these rather miserable fellows and so remounted 'The Emperor,' so named after Emperor Joseph Napoleon Bonaparte and his potty. During the Peninsula campaign under Wellington, the 14th Light Dragoons captured his baggage train at the Battle of Vitoria in 1813 which included his chamber pot. The Regiment continue to use it to toast "The Emperor" in champagne at regimental dinner nights and the Regiment has the nick name, 'The Emperor's Chambermaids'.

I then went back to sorting out the prisoners and was just about to mount up when I got a tap on my shoulder; I turned and saw a chest. Facing me was a mountain of a man, so promptly put my arms up in surrender. He laughed and said, "it's OK Sir, I am on your side". It was the Sergeant Major of The Grenadiers, our infantry. I explained we had the prisoners and that the one 'with the Radar from MASH hat,' had chucked something. I asked Lythcat for a torch and the Sergeant Major and I had a quick look in the area where the item had landed. We found a Bakelite Soviet exploder, he immediately told his soldiers to search the 'man with the Radar hat.' What happened next was incredible, to say the man was 'rag dolled' was an understatement, he was stripped in seconds and once in his underpants we could see taped to his body orange 200gm blocks of Russian TNT. He had thought about being a human bomb, thank goodness he had had second thoughts or that his detonator failed. I quickly mounted up and moved off to the BTR 60's leaving the Grenadiers to deal with the human bomb and prisoners.

Here we came across another group of Iraqis who wished to surrender to us. One caught my eye as he had a rather smart Soviet style map case that I fancied as a souvenir. I dismounted, remembering to 'cock' my pistol and took their surrender. The first thing I wanted was an AK47 to augment my rather pathetic 9mm dismounted firepower, so rather to their surprise I asked "where are your weapons? I need an AK47!" The man with the map case immediately said something in Arabic and one of the soldiers disappeared into a trench and reappeared with an AK47 with a wooden butt and four magazines. It was as this point I noticed the shoulder tabs of the man with the map case, a large eagle with crossed swords below, a Major General! I then asked him for the map case and looked inside to find it full of maps with all the positions of the Iraqi front lines marked. I got Leachy and Lythcat to search them all with Smudge covering them with the commanders GPMG and got on the radio to report a high level prisoner. Very quickly a vehicle appeared and I pointed out the prisoner, they then said, 'but he has no rank', I asked the boys where his rank slides were but got no real response, but I assured them that he was a General and he himself confirmed it. So one of my boys had a great souvenir!

Once we had dispatched the General to be interrogated I got all the other prisoners now milling around to get into an empty Iraqi tank scrape to control them better as we were only four men against about seventy. I then posted Smudge on guard with his SMG as we prepared to move out. At that moment a Grenadier Warrior motored up, so I briefed the commander that we needed to move on and could he watch the prisoners. As he had dismounted his infantry and only had a three man crew I suggested that he put the Warrior at the entrance to the tank scrape and traverse his 30mm Rarden cannon and 7.62mm Chain Gun on the prisoners. As he manoeuvred up to the entrance there was a murmur from the prisoners that degraded to shrieks of pure terror and fear as the Warrior traversed its turret to cover the prisoners. I suddenly realised what was going through the prisoners' minds and shouted to the Warrior Commander to move the gun off the prisoners. I then went forward and using sign language, tried to calm them. As I did so one prisoner came forward on his knees in the most humbling way, almost in tears saying "Please, please." I then asked him why the prisoners went crazy and he told me in halting English what we had done by putting them in a tank scrape was what the Iranians had done in the Iran-Iraq war, they then machine gunned the prisoners and buried them in the scrape. I asked him to assure the prisoners that we would not shoot them, but they must stay in the tank scrape. If they moved the crew of the Warrior would put the gun back on them.

Explaining to an Iraqi Officer that we would not shoot prisoners.

He agreed and explained to the prisoners, who started to thank me along with cries of 'Allah Akbar', or 'God is great'. Lythcat then called me and warned me that one prisoner was moving up the entrance of the scrape with a Liverpool Football Club sports bag (which in Lythcat's mind was worth shooting him for; Lythcat being a good Man U fan) and began to open it. I drew my pistol and told him to put the bag down, he slowly did so and kept saying "Thank you" but it sounded more like "spank you", which made me inwardly giggle. He asked to open the bag and did so, he then took out a book that looked like a Koran, the Islamic Bible and gave it to me. I still have it to this day. I believe it was in thanks for not killing them and treating them decently.

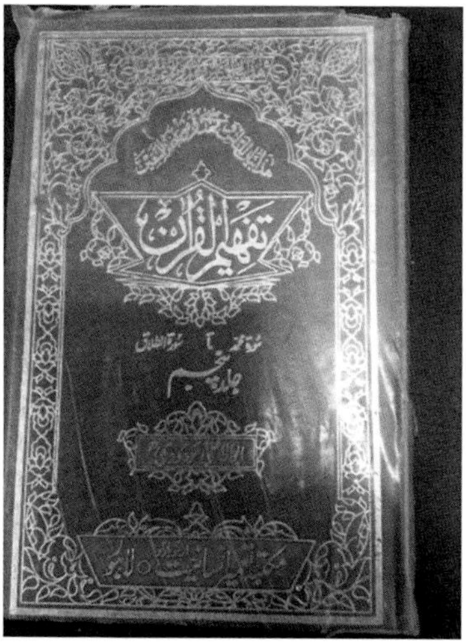

The Koranic Book.

We mounted up and continued the advance leaving the infantry with the grateful prisoners and soon were engaged shooting at some T55s while 4th troop contacted some transport that included a 'pan-technican', yes that is what Cpl Adesile called it asking for permission to engage. He was granted permission and he made the shot, there was a biggest detonation I had seen so far in the war, it must have been loaded with fuel, as it went up like a volcano and lit up the whole night.

THE FUEL BOWSER TAKEN OUT BY CPL. ADESILE
- BIG BANG!
The 'Pan-technican' Destroyed by Cpl. Adesiles Four Two.

It was at this point that in the distance we saw a mass of armour and vehicles moving north in the open and I requested Artillery support. Derek Hodson, our FOO was still back with the Sqn Leader and so could not see the target, he frantically tried to locate me on the battle field as he passed back my fire order. When he heard the golden words, 'Fire mission regiment', he went crazy ordering his driver and FOO Sergeant to find me as this was a once in a lifetime experience for any Royal Artillery officer. Just as I was about to start the fire mission, Derek roared up in his Warrior and calmly took command of what was an incredible display of firepower. An entire Regiment of M109, 155mm self-propelled guns hitting vehicles in the open was awesome. The initial ranging with one gun created some scattered explosions that soon centred on the enemy concentration. This was followed by a massive concentration of fire with the initial salvo almost arriving at the same time. The subsequent salvoes were a little more ragged but no less devastating to the exposed armour and vehicles to our front.

After these series of engagements Two Two and my tank were short on ammo and we cross-loaded some rounds from Sgt Milner on the now repaired Two One. We then swapped position with 4th Troop who now led on the front right.

We continued the advance and soon the squadron was in contact with a company minus of T55s. Richard Shirreff ordered us up into squadron line and we started to engage T55s as dawn began to break.

DESTROYED T.55. NOTE A.A. GUN
IS FACING UP. THEY BELIEVED THEY
WERE UNDER AIR ATTACK.
T55 in sand berm that offered little protection.

As we advanced into the dawn we were constantly engaging targets at extreme range and soon hit the next major objective, Copper. This is when we saw what seemed to become a pattern. We would engage between 3,500-3,000 metres from the dark side of the night sky picking off the dug in Iraqi tanks on the positions and then we would switch to the dug in infantry vehicles. The enemy would fire blindly in all directions including the air with all the weapons they had. This was initially alarming but we soon realised that it was not aimed shots, unlike our first engagement with the enemy artillery pieces.

Once the shooting on the position calmed down we advanced and assaulted allowing our infantry to clear the positions. Advancing through the position caused us some anxiety as we soon found out that they had RPGs in every trench. Some shot at us but we charged over their trenches collapsing them, so they soon gave up. Although the RPG would do little damage to a Challenger, it could still give us a mobility kill or injure us.

As we were going through one position we literally fell into a tank scrape with a massive crash throwing Lythcat forward and making me bang my head on my sight so hard I was slightly stunned. Leachy stalled the tank in the impact and as I stuck my head out to see what we had hit I saw the barrel of a T55 looking straight at me from two feet away. I grabbed our newly 'proffed' AK and blasted at the tank and surrounding area, Lythcat popped his hatch and clambered out with his SMG. I grabbed two grenades, one WP and the other fragmentation.

CPL LYTHGOE AND ME DURING THE WAR. LYTH HAS A CAPTURED AK 47.

Lythcat and myself during a lull in the fighting.

We both scrambled onto the T55 from our tank and went to the commander's hatch, Lyth prised open the hatch and I chucked both grenades in, he then slammed down the hatch. We scuttled back to our tank shouting at Leachy to get Belvoir running as the T55 was likely to explode any minute. We felt rather than heard the two concussions of our grenades and mounted up. Belvoir roared into life and we climbed out of the tank scrape and motored away. I felt the heat on the back of my neck as the T55 blew up about a minute later in a massive explosion.

As dawn rose we found ourselves assaulting a position not identified as an objective but occupied strongly with dug in T55s and MTLBs. We were soon shaking out in a frontal assault on their rear. Their tanks were firing at us over their rear decks and at a great disadvantage as their ammo storage, like our own is designed for fighting with the gun forward. It was on this position as we could see better in the breaking dawn that we could destroy the tanks by firing through the sand berm with a FIN round, about two minutes later the tank would blow up shooting it's turret into the air about thirty metres. It would then land on the desert upside down looking like a frying pan with the turret ammunition cooking off and sizzling.

Frying panned T55

The smells of battle were not what I expected, there was the cordite and scorched machine gun oil that we were used to from training, but the mixed stench of burning rubber and flesh was something that one could never prepare for. It was also mixed with the strange smell of the oil fires and the damp musty smell of our charcoal lined NBC suits.
We had donned these at the staging area before the breach, as the threat from a chemical attack was very high. These suits had one advantage; they kept us warm and reasonably dry in the drizzle that came intermittently during the night's battles. The NBC threat was still real and as we advanced, Lythcat kept his eye on the CAM detector wedged in the turret by the radios, reporting, at intervals, 'one bar sir.' The highest it got was two bars and that was as we went through the breach, three bars is time to mask up. On the occasion it reached two we had a 'bum pucker' minute or two. However as we got into close combat with the enemy the likelihood of a chemical attack dropped as even though Sadam Hussein was a complete bastard, it was unlikely that his generals would use chemical weapons in close proximity to their own troops and we also soon noticed that none were carrying their own NBC equipment.

This equipment was at best described as archaic, it was Soviet based that had a complete rubber mask that had two very small eyepieces. It was like putting a condom over your head to put on and in the heat of the desert made you sweat like a 'Belgian in a crèche'. It also completely distorted any voice commands and the rubber covered your ears, so reduced hearing as well. As dawn broke we got the message that we could reduce our NBC state, so we got out of our suits and fought on in our combats, but kept our NBC suits and gas masks very close.

A T55 hit at long range by Two Zero centre of mass.

Chapter 14
Long Range Shooting

Later in the morning we passed through a replen and bombed up with ammunition from the Squadron Quartermaster Sergeant (SQMS). I took the opportunity to grab a lot more HESH and we stacked the rounds on the turret floor. In total we probably carried an extra ten rounds on a normal full bomb load and we did not have enough room in the charge bins, so I had about five HESH charges between my legs! Not a very safe move but a risk we wanted to take, as we knew we needed more HESH and smoke. Once we were re-bombed, the Squadron Leader put us back in the front right position and very quickly we used those extra rounds. In this second period of fighting, we developed a jam in the vent tube loader. The vent tubes provide the flash that ignites the charge in the breach, these look like big brass bullet cases with no head. We dismounted the vent tube loader and dumped it on the back decks where it remained for the rest of the war. We used the reversionary mode, that involved me passing Lythcat each vent tube and he put it in place before closing the breach. It was something you practiced, but did not expect to happen but did not hamper our ability to rapid fire when the need arose showing the value of training for all eventualities.

As the battle progressed we increased our engagement ranges as our confidence in the accuracy of our gun grew and the results of our ammunition's effects on the enemy armour proved that the original 1,000-meter maximum was a huge underestimation. We were regularly recording effective hits at over 2,000 meters. This was proven very well when we engaged an MTLB at 2,400 meters on the move and initially it did not look as if we had hit it. I told Smudge that he had missed and he refuted the claim and bet me £10 that he had not. So using the 'follow the barrel' technique we kept an eye on the target and passed right by it. Sure enough, there was a neat fin round hole in its back doors and all the hatches and engine covers were blown open. Smudge won his £10 and I got this photo of it.

MTLB hit at 2,400m while firing on the move, entry hole at arrow.

The longest recorded kill was by a Gunnery Sergeant from another Squadron at over 5,000 meters.

After all this action, B Squadron was swapped over with A Squadron as we had expended a lot of ammunition and were running low. This put us in flank protection that allowed us some time to pause and dismount. As we dismounted and checked our tanks, groups of prisoners came up and surrendered. We had been informed that they were in poor morale due to not having been paid, this proved slightly wrong, they were a demoralised lot, but they had wads of cash as well as blocks of hashish. We liberated both from them as well as any weapons, including a few AK47 bayonets that were sought after prizes. Sgt Maj. 'Skip' Rae came over and confiscated all the hashish and marched off to an old trench and set fire to the lot with a jerry can of petrol. The smoke was soon billowing down wind and many a squadron soldier was drawn into the smoke, including some officers, the effects were sore eyes and a coughing fit which degraded into hilarious laughter as 'Skip' chased us all away.

We also un-earthed more weapons and I up-graded my original AK 47 with an AK-S that is the AK with a folding metal stock and Leachy got an AK-M, that has a handle protruding from the front furniture of the weapon. We also collected more magazines and ammo as well as a complete box of small black, ceramic, round grenades about the size of a golf ball. We had no idea what they were so we placed one under a rock and attached a long bit of good old army string, ensuring it was down wind, as we thought it might contain a chemical and pulled. After a delay of five seconds all that happened was a bang and a flash, we realised these were some sort of stun grenade, so we then had a competition on who could throw them the highest like boys with fire crackers, well I suppose we were just boys with fire crackers, just bigger fire crackers. At some stage 'Smudge' appeared riding a bicycle with an RPG rocket launcher shouting the lines from the movie,

'The Beast', "RPG Tank Ka-boom." This film had been a troop favourite that we had all watched as it portrayed a tank crew in the deserts of Afghanistan fighting the Mujahedeen, and to us seemed quite realistic and in fact was in many ways.

Author riding our Iraqi bike

Shortly after this we moved off, and as we did so we were soon again passing enemy positions and shooting at dug in tanks and infantry vehicles. Once again we were running low on fuel and could do with some more ammunition, so the squadron went through another replen. During the build up to war we had fitted two extra fuel drums to the back of our Challengers, similar to the Soviet T34. These were standard fifty-five gallon drums that we could push up on the back deck and fill the rear fuel cell. These had been labelled 'strategic' and so could only be used if ordered by Brigade HQ. At the replen we all washed and shaved and got ready to continue the battle, this act of washing and shaving was probably the best piece of advice I can pass on after receiving it from the Squadron Leader, he said that a wash and shave are worth four hours sleep, and he was right. The effect of this was amazing and revitalized the troop just when it was needed most. As we prepared to move off again another incident occurred that was regrettable and silly. Trooper Eddows, the driver of Two Two broke his leg while checking his tank. He was quickly evacuated by the squadron ambulance One Four Bravo, driven by Tpr Nick Baker and crewed by our Medics, Lance Corporal Walker who was a Bandsman and Private

Tait of the Royal Army Medical Corps. What was then very impressive was the arrival of Trooper Tate, a Royal Hussar battle casualty replacement (BCR) who travelled up with the Squadron Echelon and joined us within two hours of the incident.

Trooper Tate had a tough prospect joining a formed close knit unit like a tank crew and troop. We had developed the bond that is stronger than any in the world. Not only had most of us served together for years but we had all lived in close confines for months and fought together for the past two days, almost in constant contact with the enemy. The tank crew is probably the closest knit entity in the army, you know each other's habits, you know what your crew are thinking, you can read their minds, know when they are reading bad or good news from home. You know how they will respond to a practical joke or comment. You know when someone is down and needs a lift, you know who is hungry or ready to snap. You even know when people like to take a shit and know who has farted. It is without doubt the most intense of relationships and as such one that endures for life. It is a phenomenon that only soldiers who have been in combat can appreciate or understand. Trooper Tate, joined such a team, Simmo ensured he was welcomed and he did not have long to learn as we were in an engagement within two hours of him joining the troop as we attacked objective Brass and Steel. This is to a certain degree well portrayed in the recent hit movie 'Fury' where a BCR joins a US Sherman tank crew in the closing stages of WWII. We just did not have to resort to Brad Pitt's leadership styles thank goodness!

Another incident that occurred that was very strange happened as we sat in over-watch. Prisoners started to walk across the desert to us in ever increasing numbers.

Iraqi Prisoners sat behind Two Zero

They were a motley crew with not too many officers in evidence. We soon had about 50 – 75 prisoners sat on the ground behind each of our tanks, seeking shelter from the odd rounds heading in our direction from positions to our front.

Suddenly three Iraqi tanks appeared on the ridge line at about 3,500 metres moving fast towards us. We immediately closed down and engaged, each Iraqi tank being destroyed by each of mine. We immediately carried out the normal procedure after engaging the enemy, and that is to 'jockey' either left or right. A 'jockey' is a manoeuvre where you move your tank two to three hundred meters left or right after exposing your location. This involved reversing at speed until you were below the ridge or hill you were using as cover and slowly coming back up on the position trying to raise as little dust as possible. As you can imagine this was rather alarming for the prisoners sitting behind our tanks who scattered and once we settled down again after the 'jockey' hesitantly gathered once again behind our tanks. It was here that Simmo had an interesting encounter with an Iraqi. As he opened up his hatch again and went into over-watch he heard a voice with a Scouse accent. Now Simmo is in a minority group in the Regiment, he is a Scouser, most of the soldiers in the regiment are from Lancashire and Manchester. The Scouse voice he heard asked' "so what the fook happens now?" He initially thought it was one of his own crew mobbing him, until once again he heard the voice, "oy you, cloth ears, what the fook happens to us?" He soon realised that it was the young Iraqi soldier beside his tank. He called the fellow up and got his story. The poor fellow had been on holiday back in Iraq when Sadam Hussein invaded Kuwait and as a dual Iraqi/British citizen had been called up to the army. He initially had not wanted to reveal the fact that he was actually also British to us as he was convinced that he would be shot as a traitor by us. He had been persuaded by his fellow prisoners to communicate with us after nearly being run over by our 'jockeying' manoeuvre. This had rather rattled them and encouraged them to want to get out of the front line and the safely off to a POW camp. This young Iraqi was handed over to the infantry who then sent him back with the other prisoners and he was eventually repatriated to the UK. We also soon saw a column of two bridge layers and some trucks approaching, we got ready to engage but quickly recognised that they were our own engineers, a close call and one that could have ended in disaster.

A T55 brews up in its berm

Chapter 15
Fury and Fire

This pause in the fighting was to allow the Royal Scots and the Fusiliers to catch us up and for them to finish the assault on objective Steel. It was shortly after this battle that the worst single British loss of life occurred during the entire war. As the Fusiliers were forming up after the assault on the objective, with our D Squadron, they lost two Warrior fighting vehicles in two massive explosions within seconds of each other. It was at the time thought to be Iraqi mines or fire, however was later found to have been the worst case of 'Blue on Blue' of the war. Two American A10 Warthog Tank Busters had mistaken the British armour for enemy and engaged with maverick missiles completely destroying both vehicles with the loss of nine young soldiers. This included Fusilier Conrad Cole aged just seventeen, the youngest British military casualty recorded since the end of the Second World War.

At the Brigade Level it was decided to let the Fusiliers lead the advance to give them a chance to 'have a go' at the enemy and boost their morale. As a result B Squadron was detached to the Fusilier battle group and joined D Squadron who had witnessed the attack on the Warriors. D Squadron was very lucky not to get hit in the attack, as the pilots made two errors. The first was attacking friendly forces but the second was that they should have targeted the tanks first and not the infantry vehicles.

We motored over to the Fusiliers who were waiting to continue the advance. We joined them in the late afternoon and shook out into a squadron formation on the front right, with D Squadron on our left and awaited orders in sight of the smouldering wrecks of the destroyed Warriors.

With our orders received we prepared to move out. These we felt were rather flawed as the CO of the Fusiliers had chosen that his own Recce Troop with the Regimental 2IC in a Warrior should lead. At dusk we crossed the start line and saw the most impressive firepower display I had ever seen. Two regiments of MLRS (Multi Launch Rocket Systems) one UK and one US fired their complete salvos on our left and right. The ripple of destruction in the distance was awe-inspiring. This continued as we advanced with strikes on suspected enemy positions to our front. As night fell and we advanced into the dark further blackened by the oil fires. As we progressed, our superior thermal tank sights meant that we started to have to warn and guide the 'Recce screen' to our front so completely negating its use. We could see the enemy at about nine kilometres while the Recce guys of the Fusiliers could only see about a thousand or at maximum fifteen hundred meters with their Vietnam War era image intensifier sights.

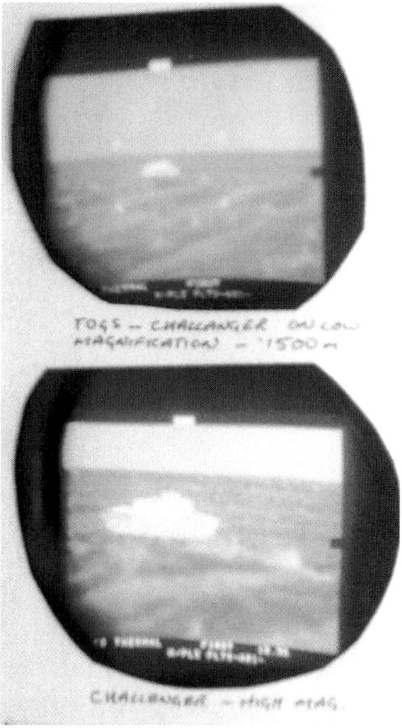

Thermal viewer of a challenger on low magnification and high.

As we talked the Recce screen onto the first targets and moved up to support them our Squadron Leader, Richard Shirreff gave us the order to pass through this ineffective screen and engage the enemy directly. We started to hit positions and soon saw a large oil facility just off our line of advance. We could also see hundreds of Iraqis retreating into the facility. We engaged them but were ordered not to damage the actual installation, which was a little annoying as there was some fire coming from it and the 'inner kid' in us all thought it would have been 'fun' to see the oil installation going boom, slightly immature I agree, but it is not often you get to shoot up such an inflammable target.

The oil infrastructure was considered sacrosanct, and as a result the advance soon halted as there was a major pipeline leading to the facility that blocked our advance. It was decided not to shoot our way through and the Engineers were called forward to bridge the obstacle. This took about an hour and was done by Combat Engineer Tractors and dozer tanks. We stood over-watch ready to engage targets that tried to interfere with the operation while the Fusiliers continued clearing bunkers and taking prisoners around us. It was here that I had to chuckle as I saw a rather pumped up Fusilier Platoon Commander herding a group of prisoners out of their bunkers between Two Zero and Two One shouting at them "why don't you bloody well fight?" and Sergeant Milner shouting over to him, "we'd rather they didn't!" Soon the crossing was open and B Squadron surged across leaving a rather miffed Platoon Commander to stew.

A defile such as this is extremely likely to be targeted by artillery or even a counter attack, so we quickly formed a ring of steel on the far side to defend against a counter attack as D Squadron and the Infantry followed to expand the bridgehead. As we moved into position 3rd Troop Leader Johnny Hollands reported passing through a Bedouin camp with tents and camels occupied by a smiling waving family. One of those indelible moments that occur in war, they were soon within our protective bridgehead as a half-hearted attempt by about six Iraqi tanks was driven off and we continued to expand the bridgehead and press on. As we pushed out the Fusilier Warriors soon started to cross and we started to shake out to continue the advance with the Squadron Leader urging us to keep moving to stop the farce of the Recce screen being re-imposed. As we moved forward I received a message that you never want to hear. "Hello Zero Bravo this is Mike Three Zero, I have been hit". Johnny sounded remarkably cool and quickly explained that he had been hit in the rear of his tank, no one was hurt but they could not move. I offered to move to his location but was assured that he was fine and we continued the advance as our REME fitter section deployed a CARRV to assess the damage and recover Johnny's tank.

During the advance we had an alarming experience that was to affect me and give me strong views on cluster munitions. We were pushing out from the bridgehead when there was an explosion under the tank. We stopped and I asked Leachy if he was ok. He said yes, so I asked him & Lythcat to check for holes, we could see none so I said let's keep going. We started to move and almost immediately there was another very loud bang, we stopped again and checked the interior of the tank, no holes, drive on. Once again we moved on and again there was a third explosion, we stopped and this time we thought we must be in an anti-personnel minefield. Lythcat and I grabbed torches and hung off the side of the tank left and right and peered into the gloom. What we saw were yellow cylinders, about the size of a coke can, I realised we were driving through one of our own cluster strikes and many had not functioned as intended. I ordered Leechy to drive on and warned the rest of the Squadron.

It was at this 'bridge' over the pipeline that Lance Corporal Ian Michael Dewsnap, plant operator of the Royal Engineers won the Military Medal. About 24 hours after we had passed over, the engineers sent a four wheeled front-end loader to improve the crossing. As he was working about 1,000 Iraqis from the main oil facility came and surrendered to him. He was slightly surprised as he only had a rifle with twenty rounds and no radio. He ordered them to form three ranks and marched them to captivity behind his digger.

It was on objective Tungsten that we had a short pause after the battle and managed to inspect some of the bunkers and Iraqi positions. Henry Joynson our Battle Captain came over and joined me and we had a chat about Johnny Hollands who was still to re-join us. His tank had been hit in its final drive and was repairable within the capabilities of the second line A2 Echelon workshop so would join us soon. We decided that we should clear a few of the bunkers after a group Iraqis emerged from a bunker about 100 meters away. We grabbed our AK 47s and started to clear the bunkers. These bunkers turned out to be quite extensive and extremely comfortable. We went in tactically and checked for any occupants. Armed with grenades, AK47s and our side arms we generally shouted a warning and if we got no response we would lob in a grenade or fire a few shots in. This process proved pretty good and we soon had cleared a number of positions. We started to clear the first bunker of what proved to be an extensive and lavish bunker complex that consisted of buried twenty and forty foot shipping containers interlinked with underground passages. As we entered the first area we found a kettle still boiling and so went into high alert.

We moved from room to room, challenging and then assaulting each room. In one, I tossed in the grenade and we heard a second bang after the grenade, Henry immediately jumped through the doorway and sprayed the room with his AK, where upon there were four returning bangs or pops. Henry jumped back out looking rather shaken, we tossed in two more grenades and both sprayed the room. We then entered to see a bank of five TV's, each with a hole in the screen, the cause of the bangs had been the tubes exploding when hit by Henry's bullets. Not a story we told too often, as we felt like a couple of right chumps. However the clearance did produce two very fine Persian carpets that we rolled up and put on Henry's Battle Wagon.

Henry Joynson in a command bunker

We took a number more prisoners who seemed to be well supplied with hashish and cash. We confiscated blocks of hashish that were wrapped in thin black plastic and bundles of Iraqi Dinars in twenty-five Dinar note denomination that had Sadam's face on as well as ten and five Dinar notes. We gathered all the hashish and cash, the hashish was once again gathered by Skip Rae the SSM and burnt. This time we did not all shuffle downwind to see if we could inhale the smoke and have some fun. The cash on the other hand, was split up amongst all the crews so they all had a souvenir from Iraq with the 'great' leader's mug on it. We also found a safe in one bunker that we blew open in a rather ‘Keystone’ cops fashion that sent notes floating round the place and basically singed and burnt them all.

Chapter 16

Charge to Hell's Highway

We got the word to move out and reformed for the advance east towards the vaunted Wadi Al Batin. This was expected to be a major obstacle to the advance into Kuwait and we planned to cross it at the site of some quarries.

As we advanced we were given orders not to bother and stop to round up prisoners, but to destroy all armour and vehicles in our path and expect to come across lines of vehicles of retreating Iraqis heading back to Basra. This then became a massive classic cavalry charge across the desert. When we came across surrendering Iraqis we simply stood up in our cupolas and pointed them to the rear.

As we crested a major ridgeline we saw a convoy of vehicles stretching from south to north moving north. The squadron leader brought all available tanks up onto the ridge and A Squadron moved up on our left as well. This was going to be a turkey shoot and Richard Shirreff started to give orders on what vehicles to take out first and arranging for a ripple of fire from left to right, starting with 1st troop. As he described targets, BMPs on flanks and a ZSU-23-4 that was assigned to my tank. He then said once we had destroyed any armour we should destroy the trucks and other vehicles. As he continued to give orders for the destruction of this massive convoy I observed and tracked my target with my gunner, Smudge. Something with the picture was not right and we started to look at the other vehicles and study their thermal signatures. In the thermal sight my target looked like a ZSU in that it had a turret and there seemed to be a radar dish on the back of the turret that was emitting far more heat than the rest of the vehicle except the engine and exhaust. As we watched the radar dish 'got off' and had a piss. On the thermal sight the stream of pee is easily seen. I immediately called Zero Alpha (Richard) and informed him of this, we then looked harder and the trucks started to look familiar. Sadly before he could send the message through to Regimental Headquarters and A Squadron, two tanks from A Squadron opened fire on the 'BMPs' and we saw the impacts on two flanking vehicles that exploded in a fireball. Almost immediately a check-fire command came over the net. A Squadron had destroyed two Spartan Armoured vehicles of an Air Defence Regiment. They had been protecting 7th Armoured Brigades Artillery Echelon that had decided to take a short cut across our line of advance instead of following the main supply route through our rear. The dust from the convoy and the heat haze made identification difficult. This case of 'blue-on-blue' demonstrated once again how in the fog of war mistakes are made and lives lost. Bravely, an A Squadron officer drove down to the site in his challenger, climbed out the turret and stood on the front wing and was surrounded by a large group of bewildered soldiers. He then said something along the lines of, "Err sorry, bit of a blue-on-blue, is everyone OK? Is there anything we can do?" where upon a voice from the back in a thick Scots accent said, "Nay, just fook off" so he responded, "rightio then, I'll be off" climbed into his hatch and motored back up the hill. So in a fashion the situation had been resolved. However there were casualties sadly and the injured soldiers evacuated to the field hospital and we resumed our headlong charge to Kuwait.

The advance continued into the night with intermittent contacts and we once again were running low on ammunition and requiring fuel. A pause was at last ordered and we carried out another 'replen' and formed up for a short move to a leaguer area. Here the effect of exhaustion made its mark and I experienced a potentially disastrous incident that still gives me nightmares... As we waited for the complete Squadron to filter through the 'replen' the lack of sleep and constant movement and fighting took its toll. Very quickly my crew and I fell asleep, as did many of the other crews. A knocking on my helmet woke me, there stood Cpl Simpson with the words, "for fucks sake Sir, the rest of the squadron has moved off." I think my first thought was 'oh shit' and immediately woke the rest of the crew. I told Simmo to go to all the tanks behind us and make sure everyone was awake and that we were moving off. He did so and reported back to me. We then moved off realising I had no idea where we were going, I did not have a GPS and even if I did, I did not have a grid reference to plot. So I told my gunner to follow the hot track marks of the Squadron Leader and 2IC who had headed off without us. I then told Leachy, the driver to follow the gun barrel. This is a technique we used when you wanted to go in particular direction towards an enemy position but needed to flank them. The Gun will stay on the point the gunner lays it on and the hull moves as required below it. As we were following tracks that were fast getting cold, the gun was pointed about twenty feet in front of the tank. I was told later by my troop Sergeant, Sgt Milner behind me that we looked like a giant ant-eater, sniffing the ground with our long snout! We quickly caught up with the Squadron Leader and 2IC, who were blissfully unaware of the complete 'cock up' that had played out behind them and the near loss of his entire squadron. (Sorry Richard, this is probably the first time you heard about this). We soon formed into a leaguer and posted guards and got the order to get some sleep and a wash, we had four hours and would move out again at dawn. As there was still fighting in the area and we could see artillery exchanges taking place I ordered my troop to sleep under our tanks or in their crew positions, for those under the tanks I ordered that they have their gas masks, weapons and also to wear their helmets. The drivers all kipped down in their seats but most of us crawled under our steeds. I was asleep in an instant in my helmet and it seemed like I had only been asleep for five minutes when I was woken up by a tug on my foot. I immediately sat bolt upright and straight back down again as my helmet cracked into the belly armour of the tank. I was very grateful to my earlier experience at the start of the air war and my order to wear helmets. Not the case for most the other troop members who had not heeded my order to wear their helmets and now sported neat round blue eggs on their foreheads.

We shook ourselves out of slumber and resumed the advance in Squadron column with all tanks except Pommer's tank, One Zero. Johnny was back with us as was Zero Bravo, Richard's tank that had broken down earlier in the advance. We approached the Wadi Al Batin and soon crossed in haze that reduced visibility to 1000 meters. As we climbed out of the Wadi we came across a T59 (Chinese copy of a T55) and a BMP 2 racing across our front heading north.

Last target of the war, BMP shot by Two Zero

I engaged the BMP and hit it about a foot from the rear. Simmo in Two Two engaged the T59 and hit it a glancing blow on the front left, hitting a stowage bin.

Both halted and about five to six Iraqis jumped out of the T59 (a tight fit for a tank designed for a crew of four) and about ten from the BMP who ran into the desert to hide.

We soon came up on them, rounded up the prisoners who turned out to all be officers and stopped to see what we could 'proff' from the vehicles. Simmo grabbed the 14.7mm machine gun off the T59 and the crew helmets (schlemafon). We searched the BMP and grabbed the schlemafon and an AK47 bayonet. As we were getting out of the vehicle a Heckler Koch MP5 sub-machine gun fell out of a blanket roll. This was a prized trophy, and we soon had a go firing it as it fired the same ammo as our Nine Millies and SMG's.

Last Target hit by Two Two, T59

We heard over the net that a ceasefire was imminent and planned for 08.00. We halted on a ridgeline at 07.15 and at 08.30 we got the confirmation that the war was over. We all dismounted and high-fived each other shook hands and hugged.

It seemed that 2nd Troop had fired the first and last rounds for the Regiment in this war. The first main armament tank rounds under Regimental command since 1945 and the last as the 14th/20th Kings Hussars as the Regiment amalgamated with the Royal Hussars in 1993 forming The Kings Royal Hussars.

Photo taken at 08.00 27th February 1991 on the ceasefire

Evening Standard

Bush orders ceasefire after 100 hours of war

Saddam tells Iraqis to lay down arms

VICTORY!

The Evening Standard's fair summary

Chapter 17
Aftermath

The feeling of elation was incredible, mixed with relief and fatigue. We were on a high, and I took photos of my crew with our AK47s and Cpl Baugley, the Driver of Zero Bravo came over for a photo as well. We also then unfurled flags and flew them from our antennas. I had an interesting array, a Norwegian flag and a South Korean. The Norwegian one was for my closest childhood friend and the South Korean was sent by the Korean veteran of 2nd Troop B Squadron who sent me the tank names. We then mounted the 14.7mm Russian gun on my tank using the flag holder and had a 'blat'. It dwarfed our own 7.62mm GPMG.

12.7mm from the T59 on Two Zero, note the size of our GPMG below it

After staying in position for a couple of hours we got orders to move further into Kuwait to set up a squadron leaguer, unload our guns and tank cannons. Unloading a 120mm tank cannon is not that easy as the round is wedged pretty firmly in the breach. You basically have to stab the bag charge in the most sensitive area of the propellant if FIN or DU is loaded and drag it out, you then have to use the tank cleaning rods to tap the round out by pushing them down from the muzzle. Not too bad if FIN or DU is loaded but a little more worrying if HESH is loaded as basically you are tapping on the nose of a live round with a fuse. Then went to sleep and slept for a straight 12 hours.

DAWN AFTER THE WAR – WE SLEPT FOR
12 HOURS.

Tank Bivi's on the sides of our tanks the morning after the war ended, Simmo doing his teeth.

We then moved again, closer to Kuwait city and once in our new location plans were made to bring up our Echelons and the supplies to make a more permanent camp.

During this process the Regiment suffered its worst single loss of personnel. A work party was gathered and loaded onto four trucks to go back to Al Jubail and collect our personal kit that we had left before deploying on our tanks. As they travelled down they stopped for a break and while a group were taking a pee, one soldier picked up a cluster bomb, not knowing what it was he tossed it into the desert where it exploded and injured John Walton, John Orrel and Gaz Foss from Recce Troop who was hit in the bum. The jokes were made that he was never the fastest runner and unjustifiable about being a double arsehole. They were evacuated and our kit eventually reached us a few days later than expected. This certainly focused our minds on the fact that the dangers of war were still with us in the form of mines and ERW (Explosive Remnants of War), something I was to become very involved in after leaving the army.

During the war, we fired all the types of ammunition supplied by the UK Army for the 120mm rifled gun. This included HESH, Smoke, FIN and DU (Depleted Uranium). There has been much debate about the effects of DU on the troops linked to 'Gulf War Syndrone'. I know of two members of the $14^{th}/20^{th}$ Kings Hussars who suffered 'Gulf War Syndrome' as it became known including our own medic Lance Corporal Walker. I am not sure that it is linked to the DU rounds but more likely linked to the cocktail of vaccinations, drugs (NAPS), pollution and other stresses that we were exposed to against medical advice. Pommers actually put his radiation monitoring device, a small dark grey disc worn as a watch on your right wrist on a DU Round in his tank, he was never evacuated for radiation poisoning after the monitor was read. We found the DU an extremely effective round and it was deadly on enemy tanks at extreme range with first shot accuracy often through the sand berms that were there to protect them. We took stock of our ammunition status, and found that we had fired two and a half bomb loads in Two Zero. Two Two had used about two bomb loads and Two One, one bomb load. We had also fired over 8,000 rounds of 7.62mm from our two machine guns and two hand grenades in Two Zero.

THE EFFECT WE HAD ON THE IRAQI TANKS.
PENETRATION ON A T.55.

The effect of DU and FIN on a T55 (Photo: Stephen Bryant)

Within a week of the end of the war, a group of boffins turned up and started to interview the crews of every tank involved in the war. They started with the crews of 7 Brigade and then came to us. As we chatted about the modifications we had made to our tanks and the experiences we had had fighting our tanks they became more and more interested and asked to be shown the various modifications such as the extra stowage in our engine compartment allowing for under-armour stowage of the drivers tools, the torch from the British Legion that I and Simmo had stuck on the backside of our sights. They also started to interrogate us about how many tanks, APCs and other vehicles we had destroyed. They were amazed at our ammunition expenditure and checked our fire control computer for barrel wear due to the number of rounds fired. It showed that barrel wear was significant but in line with the expected norms. When they totalled up the numbers they informed me that 2nd Troop B Squadron, 14/20H had fired more rounds than the whole of 7th Armd Brigade combined. Two Zero and Two One had fired more rounds than the Queens Royal Irish Hussars and Two Two and

Two One had fired more than the Scots Dragoon Guards! I was in shock, we knew we had had a busy war, but no busier than anyone else.

Once we knew all was well and hostilities had truly ceased we took out some patrols, initially with our tanks, but quite quickly changed to soft skinned vehicles and some old Land Rovers from abandoned Iraqi positions. On the first patrols we gathered two tents, which were small marquees. We used them as our troop accommodation and even found some beds with iron bedsteads for the boys who did not have an US army cot. Possibly one of the best bits of equipment we recovered was a Soviet era cook trailer. It had two large soup kettles and ran on wood, diesel or petrol. The LAD soon got it running and we filled it with water, this allowed us to have hot showers and shaving water in the desert.

OUR CAMP AFTER THE WAR. — CAPTURED IRAQI TENTS.

2nd Troop Camp in the Kuwaiti Desert

These patrols provided both a release and distraction from boredom but also served a purpose. We went out and took the surrender of Iraqi stragglers and we also marked and recorded locations were fallen Iraqis lay. This was a sad job and made us realise the suffering this war had caused for ordinary Iraqi families. On one position we found a number of Iraqis who had been caught in their vehicles. Sitting in the cabs of their trucks. As we approached on foot Leachy kicked a boot that was sticking out of the desert, as it spun through the air a foot flew out! With a shriek Leachy turned white. I nearly threw up and we did not know whether to laugh or cry. We tried to show respect to these poor souls and recorded the locations so that the grave digging parties could bury the Iraqi dead and try and record whom these fallen soldiers were so their next of kin could be informed. Although it was gruesome task, it gave some fulfilment as we all felt a great affinity with these unfortunate soldiers who had not been as lucky as us. The least we could do was to provide them some dignity in death. This was not always the case, and some fellow officers had to caution some soldiers for silly actions, such as taking photos with a corpse in a truck cab, or sticking a cigarette in the mouth of a corpse.

We soon had a team that made these excursions into the desert. We had two Land Rovers, one open top and the squadron Land Rover. Henry Joynson and I travelled in one with Leachy driving. The other we filled with those who were interested to join us. Initially another officer joined us, but unfortunately on the second or third day of the patrols he had a mishap with his 'Nine Millie'. We were preparing to head out he was checking his pistol when he had a negligent discharge and put a round into the sand. That put paid to his fun days out and he ended up giving a sizable contribution to the Army Benevolent Fund. To offset this mishap I shared my one bottle of port with him that I had received in a Fortnum & Mason hamper sent by an old school friend Marcus Hill. He and my old dorm mates had decided what a gentleman should campaign with: Patum Peperium, water biscuits, stilton and other delicacies. He had managed to plonk the bottle in when the cashier was not looking, an act against the rules imposed on F&M by the Army, a rule that in my view was ludicrous and unnecessary.

On these missions we also collected enemy equipment, information and looked for souvenirs as well as looking for more soft skinned vehicles for our own use and spares for our Land Rovers. We travelled in a wide arc finding devastation in all directions. A column of 2S1 self-propelled 152mm artillery guns destroyed on a road by airpower and other positions seemingly untouched but abandoned. On one such position we found six 37 mm automatic air defence guns (M1939 (61-K)). They were laid out in berms with bunkers and crew positions. All were loaded and we felt they would make a great Squadron trophy. Henry and I climbed on one and tried to work out how to unload the five round clip that was in each gun. I sat on one side and Henry the other as we pulled levers and the breach mechanism nothing seemed to move the rounds. I think the next bit went a bit like this…. "Henry, what do you think this peddle does?" "I don't know, try it," so I stamped down on the peddle and the gun barked five times! Henry and I looked at each other and he said, "well that seems to have unloaded it!" We looked as the shells impacted harmlessly in the open desert about 4 kilometres away and decided it was time to get out of this sector without our trophy. The following morning at the daily situation briefing, there was an interesting report in the enemy actions part of the brief. Five rounds of incoming were reported in the American sector. Henry and I looked at each other and kept very quiet feigning complete innocence.

We soon were ranging up to fifty kilometres from our base in the desert and reaching the outskirts of Kuwait City. This meant passing through the Egyptian sector where Henry and I had an entertaining time with the Egyptians drinking tea and being offered 200 cigarettes if we left the young blonde blue eyed REME Fitter who was with us for a couple of hours. Apparently the Egyptian Colonel had taken a fancy to him!

Don't you dare leave me, Sir!??

On this trip we entered Al Jahra Air Base. A former Kuwaiti Air Force base that had been bombed to bits, literally. The bunkers were collapsed and every building bearing some kind of damage, except the Mosque. We came across a unit of RAF Regiment NBC Recce there with the Green Jacket Major who had given us the camouflage briefing at Sennelager. The RAF guys were convinced that we were SAS, mistaking our Shite Hawk cap badge for a flying dagger, this was possibly reinforced by the fact that we all had shoulder holsters and carrying AK47's and a Heckler Koch MP5A. Anyway, the up side of this little mistake was that they opened up their stores wagon and let us help ourselves to anything we wanted, and boy did we! Hot chocolate, apple pudding, cheese, waterproofs and all manner of goodies that the RAF get and we never knew existed.

On one of the first days of travelling around we went up to the Mutla Ridge and saw the devastation of the 'Highway of Death or Hell's Highway.' It was difficult to take in. We arrived about a week after the ceasefire and the day after the engineers had cleared the highway by bulldozing the destroyed Iraqi vehicles off the road. Even then, some engines were still running and dead Iraqis still in their cabs and crew positions of their tanks, BMPs, SP guns and armoured cars.

Mutla Ridge Police Post, Soviet 2S1 Self Propelled Gun on left

There were civilian cars, trucks, busses and military vehicles. Some were luxury models including a Range Rover, that we dismantled for spares for a V8 Land Rover that we found at the top of the Mutla Ridge opposite the police post. We towed this back and got it running with the spares from the Range Rover. This increased our fleet and gave us more mobility, as we could not always use the squadron Land Rover as it was needed for other duties.

As we headed down the hill from the police post on the Mutla Ridge three women in a black limousine flagged us down. They were all young Kuwaitis and so we pulled over on the hard shoulder of the motorway. They asked us over and Henry and I went over to say hello. They thanked us for liberating them and asked us to come to their car. Both Henry and I had had no idea what to expect and one thought certainly went through my mind that reminded me of the RAMC Sergeant Majors chat in Sennelager, but as they opened the car door, they showed us a very fine Persian carpet, which they said was a gift from them to us for liberating them.

Iraqi V8 Land Rover used by B Sqn

We loaded it into the Land Rover and headed back to our Bedouin camp. We now realised we had three great carpets, two from the Iraqi bunker and now this one that was huge, all would look great in the mess back in Germany. I later saw them with the Regiment in the operational mess in Bosnia!

Leechy and Hindmoor with the other Iraqi Landy

We also met up with a Troop of Kuwaiti armoured soldiers. They were equipped in a troop of four tanks. Three Yugoslav T72's and a Chieftain 900, a variant of the old British Chieftain. What was interesting was they all wanted to be in the Chieftain which was the troop leader's tank and was one of the fourteen that managed to escape from Kuwait during the initial invasion.

Kuwaiti T72

Possibly one of the best days after the war was when we were given the opportunity to do an exchange visit with the 2nd Armoured Cavalry Regiment of the US Army. This had been arranged by Richard Shirreff and involved them visiting us and then us flying over to their position in a Black Hawk helicopter. The Yanks visit to us was fun and they had a chance to drive our challengers, Henry's 432, the LO's Ferret and a Land Rover. Our return visit started with the flight in the Black Hawk back along our line of advance. Ian Thomas gave the pilots the GPS readings of all our contacts and objectives and we flew along the path of our advance. The most amazing sight was the battle of Al Hanniah, a location that meant little to me but was the talk of all in the rest of the Regiment. On the night of the 26th February an Iraqi mixed T55 and T62 Brigade came across our line of advancc from the north. The Regiment was brought up into line and engaged in a massive turkey shoot of these enemy tanks as they tried to counter the invasion. On my side (the far right) we destroyed about ten tanks and so it was no busier than the other nights of combat. 2nd Troop was basically tidying up the stragglers that had managed to weather the storm of fire from the rest of the Regiment. However, from the air we could see the scope of the battle and the number of Iraqi tanks we had destroyed.

Most interesting to Simmo, Sgt Milner and I was the over flight of the first contact of the war where we were nearly hit. It proved to be a position with three artillery guns that we though looked like South African made 155mm G5s in a position protecting the BTR 60 location that was the Iraqi Artillery Major General's HQ. We could see our track marks round the gun positions and also the craters from their fire on our positions.

BTR 60 PB destroyed by 2nd Troop in first engagement

G5 155mm artillery gun that engaged 2nd Troop over open sights on first night of the war. Note it is in direct fire mode.

The rest of the day was a bit of a blur as the magnitude of our achievement registered at the number of destroyed enemy armour left on the battlefield. One event I do remember, was when I was invited to drive an Abrams tank commanded by Lt. Bob Mark. I jumped into the drivers cab and initially did a neutral turn and nearly threw the track. We then set off across the desert and picked up speed. As we approached a sand ridge Bob asked me to slow down and I did the 'two footed' brake stamp used on Challenger. The Abrams has a far superior set of brakes and as a result it felt like the tank stood on its nose. We carried on round the area looking at the vast display of America hardware leaguered in the desert. On our return to Bob's platoon position I climbed out to thank him and noticed he had a bloody lip and swollen eye. Simmo was waving a finger at me as I apologised and tried to explain the Challenger braking drill.

One night the Regiment hosted a Regimental Band concert and dinner for the Battle Group, Brigade and Divisional staff. It started with the Regimental Band led by Bandmaster Hicks beating the retreat around a captured T55. This included a rendition of a Regimental favourite, the 'Post Horn Gallop' played through the barrel of the T55 that was traversed around the audience. It was great fun and just such a surreal experience. We were blessed with probably one of the best Regimental bands in the army with an extremely gifted band master and an unbelievable set of Bandsmen who had all manned the Squadron ambulances and the Regimental Aid Post during the war. All were highly trained brave medics who in peacetime provided the regiment with some excellent entertainment. The Padre, Captain Michael Weymes had procured booze for the evening with a run down to Bahrain and it was in plentiful supply. One down side was that once again the Subalterns were not invited to the actual dinner as there was not enough space. On chatting to the Padre I discovered that there was deemed to be only enough wine and beer in supply to be served at dinner, so the spirits were not going to be used for the guests. I persuaded him to give me the 'buckshee' spirits for an alternative Subalterns party. We gathered on the sand berm surrounding the concert location and adjacent to the tents where the dinner was being held overlooking the band, who continued to play and entertain during dinner. To give us light we cracked open a complete box of cylumes (Chemical light sticks). I think it was Ed Gimlette who split one open and discovered that the liquid continued to glow when put on the sand, skin or clothing. He then flicked me with 'cylume juice' and this soon degenerated into a full-scale fight with luminous liquid being flicked all over the place. Some of the band joined in the hilarity and very soon we were all glowing in the dark. However Mr Hicks was not very amused and so chased us off. As we headed back over the desert to our troop locations I looked over and saw glowing human forms staggering their way to bed. The next morning was particularly hard and there were a number of very sore heads, including my own which was not helped as I was summoned yet again to explain to the Adjutant why I had sprayed the band with cylume juice.

One of the fun aspects of our patrols was also to recover serviceable enemy vehicles. Our remit was to recover any vehicles, in particular armoured vehicles to the EECP (Enemy Equipment Collection Point) to ensure that the Iraqi Army did not recover them later. There were also theories that the vehicles would be shipped to Canada at the British Army Training Unit Suffield to act as the opposition force (Opfor) on the exercises that we conducted there. The main fun was the fact that we got to drive these vehicles back to the EECP. This certainly ended up in some races and in many cases some 'dodgems'. It was an incredible crash when two 40-ton tanks clashed and tried to bump each other. We did get some odd looks from the guys at the EECP when they saw the damage to the tanks. As part of the fun, A Squadron Leader, Peter Garbutt arranged for a range to be set up where we could fire enemy weapons. This included a serviceable T55 and all weapons down to Iraqi officer's pistols.

One day in this period we were ordered to report to the EECP for the visit of The Chief of the Defence Staff Sir David Craig. As we gathered, there were officers from all the Regiments in the Brigade including a group from the Fusiliers. This included the Platoon Commander of the platoon responsible for shooting Johnny Hollands' final drive after crossing the pipeline. Interestingly, Johnny knew him as they had been at RMA Sandhurst together and so when he started to make a joke of the incident and describe it as funny, Johnny stepped up and punched him, we grabbed Johnny as the platoon commander got up off his bum and kept them apart. The Divisional Commander rushed over to find out what the ruckus was about as Sir David was only two contingents up the line. When we told him, he said, "fair cop, carry on", and to the Fusilier platoon commander, "sort out your AFV recognition".

Back at the camp, we had established quite a Bedouin Sheiks palace. We had the two marquees, a mess area with a sofa and a comfy chair and Trooper Tate had made a subterranean den. We had a great kitchen with a double burner and some Iraqi army pots and pans that made for great troop nosh sessions. We set up a pretty smart shower block with the Iraqi cook trailer close by, so ensuring that B Squadron had warm showers and hot shaving water. We never let our cooks cater for us and avoided all fresh rations.

One of the other oddities was the issue of water money. In January someone worked out that all the troops from Germany were actually losing money while on active duty. In Germany we got LOA, Local Overseas Allowance, which for a single soldier was about £2 a day. After being out of Germany for thirty days we lost this allowance and unlike the US Army, the British Army did not pay combat pay. The greatest to suffer were those with families as they also lost the extra allowances for their families left behind in Germany. To try and rectify this crazy bureaucratic cockup the army instigated a water allowance that paid us £3.50 a day, however it had to be administered in theatre, so the paymaster came and arranged for us all to open Post Office Savings accounts. Our allowance was then paid in direct. Quite strange, but we were not complaining as it was a significant income for us all. We now had an opportunity to access these funds with a trip to the Forces Field Post Office, and as we were told that we would soon be going back to Al Jubail we drew out some cash. During this period of waiting, Peter Garbutt, A Squadron Leader in the Gulf who had commanded C Squadron, the Berlin Armoured Squadron before the war started to pick his troop leaders, and he was offered his pick of officers by the Colonel, I was thrilled when he chose Johnny and I for this plum posting.

As the day of departure from the desert loomed the order went out to hand in all captured enemy weapons as they were to be registered and the best ones identified for return to the Regiment as souvenirs for display in Squadron Offices and the messes of the regiment. We were asked to gather all the squadrons captured weapons and ammunition at the SHQ. It was an impressive haul, over 150 weapons of all types, rifles, pistols, sub-machine guns, RPG launchers, AK 47s in all variations, an automatic grenade launcher and a number of 12.7 and 14.7 mm heavy machine guns, not bad from a squadron of about 100 men. This haul included the Heckler Koch MP5A that we had liberated from the BMP at the end of the war.

Author with the captured weapons haul

It was hoped that this would become the Colonel's driver's weapon for the future. Unfortunately this never happened and we do not know what happened to this gun. On our return to Germany, some 6 months later a delivery was made to the Regiment in York Barracks and each Mess got a weapon for display.

4th Armoured Brigade on Parade

The move back to Saudi Arabia and plans for shipping home soon started to be realised.

D Squadron was nominated to join the stabilization force to be based in Kuwait for a further two months as they had enjoyed Christmas at home. Before D Squadron departed the Brigade arranged a Brigade photo that was allegedly taken by a Recce Tornado and from a helicopter. As we formed up in a suitable empty part of the desert the Regimental Band marched up and down the lines of tanks and APCs to entertain us.

The Regimental Band entertains!

Chapter 18
Back to Solid Ground

As D Squadron departed, we offered them most of our kit, and they grabbed our beds, tents and other goodies including the B Squadron Iraqi cook trailer. As they went past us, we loaded their tanks up and they ended up looking like a gypsy's caravan train. We also packed down our camp and prepared to move back to Saudi. We loaded the tanks onto transporters and moved by 4-ton trucks to an airstrip that had been carved out of the desert by the engineers. As we waited we saw a New Zealand Air Force C130 land and take A Squadron back to Al Jubail. Next in came an RAF C130 for us. The ground controller started to guide the aircraft in the dispersal and we could all see that he was directing the aircraft to turn with the slope. The pilot chose to ignore the ground controller and turn up hill. This caused the nose wheel to dig in. The pilot then redeemed himself by giving us an amazing display of the power of the C130. Using reverse thrust and forward thrust, he wheelied the aircraft round and turned it around. We picked up our kit and trooped on the aircraft taking our seats on the canvas slings that act as seating in a C130 for the short flight to Al Jubail. We landed and were taken back to Black Adder lines, the place where it all started. It had changed little since December, and still had the shower blocks and tents, just more of them. Richard Shirreff informed us that we would go for supper at the Al Jubail Hilton to celebrate, so we should get our best combats on and spruce up for a night of real food.

We got a lift in to town in a Land Rover and piled out at the hotel, rather surprising the immaculately turned out doorman. We shuffled into the marble floored foyer, I say shuffled, as we were unused to walking on solid surfaces. It was odd as we had spent the last 94 days walking on sand. As we were shown into the Steak House we noticed a long table set up in the middle of the dining room laid out for about 20. We were shown in to a table in the corner and settled down for a feast. As our starters were being delivered a group of officers came in and started to sit down noisily at the long table, most were lieutenant colonels with a smattering of majors, four full colonels and two brigadiers all wearing the 'Black Adder' badge of the Divisional Rear Echelon support. They soon noticed us and it was interesting to see how they quietened down after some initial disparaging looks at this scruffy bunch sat in the corner and the realisation of who we were. It was nice to see how the rear echelon dined during the war.

The next day our tanks arrived and we went down to de-kit them and unload them of all the ammunition and extras prior to shipment back to Germany. This initially involved driving through a loop with stands for each item that had to be unloaded. The first was the main armament ammunition. Here we were told to unload and put the ammunition and charge bags into containers. For 2nd Troop this took about 10 minutes as we did not have much to give back. The RAOC guys manning the stand could not believe it as they told us that most 7 Brigade tanks came back with full bomb loads. We then handed in our machine gun ammunition and 9mm ammo. We had an unexpected surprise at the next stand where we had to unbolt our ERA from the front of the Tank. As we unbolted it and placed it in the containers we noticed that we had three plates that had activated. These were right underneath on the left hand side. We were unsure if this had been from the close call on the first night or from the cluster munitions that had exploded on the second night of the war or some other close call that we had not noticed in the confusion of battle. In anyway, it gave us some food for thought.

We then off loaded our food and personal kit which included some great souvenirs. I managed to collect some Iraqi helmets, two AK bayonets, two other bayonets, a 152mm-shell case and a map case. Others had Iraqi berets, Iraqi uniforms and other kit, but no weapons. The final act was taking the tanks through a wash down to get all the muck off. We were lucky in that we just had to get the wagons clean, the Americans had to completely fumigate their vehicles and ensure all soil and sand was out of the vehicles as they had very strict rules on soil and plant matter being imported to the US. Once done we bid farewell to Belvoir, Bellman and Beeswing never to see them again. This was sad, as during the fighting, smudge had scratched a mark on the breach for each enemy tank, APC and vehicle we had destroyed, which was our record. Apparently 2nd Troops tanks were sent off to the Armoured Vehicle Research Agency for testing, as they were the most engaged tanks of the British Division and Two Two went back to being a Challenger 2 test-bed.

Once completed, we headed back to Black Adder lines and were granted some 'runs ashore' as the navy would call it in Al Jubail town. The town had become a veritable war tourist centre, every shop was selling tee shirts with cartoons of Camels and tanks, logos such as "Holy War" said by Sadam with a tank charging across the desert and Sadam saying "Holy Shit". There were also the usual trinkets found in the Gulf before the war, stuffed camels, Bedouin dishdash, knives and headdress. You could even pose on a camel for a photo. Johnny and I passed by a barbers shop, as it had been a long time since my 'US Marine flat top' I felt it would be great to get a trim and a cutthroat shave. We went in and were made extremely welcome by the owner who spoke little English. We explained through sign language what we wanted. We were sat down and started to relax and enjoy the pampering, the shave was great and the hair wash divine, what happened next was not so fun. As we sat there the old man cutting my hair started to pluck my eyebrows with a thread, and it hurt, a lot! The next thing got both me and Johnny reaching for our guns and was so unexpected that we nearly shot the barbers. They took a big cotton bud, dipped it in some liquid and before we knew what was happening they set fire to the cotton bud and in my case this flaming object was shoved up my nose and in Johnny's it was shoved in an ear. We both leapt up and reached for our pistols that were in our shoulder holsters. The poor barber started to beg for his life and there was quite a commotion. From the back of the shop ran a young lady who had heard the commotion and asked what was happening in English. I explained we had been assaulted and explained our shock at having burning cotton buds in our facial orifices. She burst out laughing and explained that this was the normal way to remove hair from these places in the Arab world. We apologised, drank the tea offered and beat a hasty retreat.

Soon after getting back to Al Jubail, Ian Thomas was taken ill and rushed off to the Norwegian Field Hospital. Richard Shirreff sent me off to see how he was doing, knowing that I spoke Norwegian, so I headed off accompanied by Henry and Johnny, all fantasising about meeting some Nordic beauties, we were to be sadly disappointed, the whole hospital only contained male nurses and staff bar one ferocious matron. Needless to say Tommo did not get many more visitors and survived his experience with his honour intact.

Finally we were given our departure date, the 1st April, so early that morning we were bussed down to Dhahran airport where we were searched at least twice and our bags X-rayed for weapons by the RMP. All my souvenirs made it through but I had to argue about the bayonets, this was eventually solved when I explained that we all had them and many of us deployed with knives that were larger than the very bayonets we were taking back with us. Once we were checked in we moved through to the departure lounge and sat down to wait for boarding. After a couple of hours the Captain of the British Airways Jumbo Jet came in and explained the delay. A catering truck driver had knocked the emergency slide off the planes main door, as a result the aircraft if not repaired would have to depart with 100 less passengers. Furthermore, if the door could not be fixed before 11.30 the aircraft would not be able to leave until 4pm once the air temperature had dropped. He also told us that 'Abdul' the catering truck driver had been given the option to resign or come and apologise to us, he chose to resign. Literally with minutes to spare a door was flown in from Riyadh and we were rushed on board. The officers were all sat in First Class and I had seat 1A with Johnny in 1B right at the front of the plane. The senior ranks (Sergeant Majors and Sergeants) were in business class and the corporals and soldiers in economy. The crew were great and we all had two drinks served before we had taxied to the end of runway and as soon as we were up in the air the drinks trollies were in full swing. A couple of hours into the flight a huge roar came from the back of the plane that was easily audible in first class. Col Vickery asked me to go back and see what was happening. Business class was deserted and as I went through the curtain to the Economy section there was a British Airways stewardess taking off her shirt! I asked her what was going on, she smiled broadly and said it was an auction. The crew were swapping their uniforms for ours. It all started when one of the Stewardesses had asked for one of the soldier's berets and so he had said I'll swap it for your hat, and so it developed and soon a striptease was going on with soldiers sitting wearing BA Shirts, hats and skirts while the BA crew sported Desert camouflage shirts, trousers, berets and belts. I realised that this might be a problem when we landed in Hanover as there was expected to be a lot of press to meet our flight. James Hewitt was on board and the whole Diana affair had broken in the press while we were in the Gulf. All the tall officers had been briefed to surround Jamie as we came off the plane and on to the buses to hide him, in the event, due to our late departure we arrived at 1am on a wet German night with not a journalist in sight.

We travelled back to Munster in coaches and arrived back in York Barracks at dawn to be met by Susie Vickery, the Colonel's wife, who kissed us all as we came off the bus.

As I greeted her I dropped an absolute clanger, I said, "Oh wow, congratulations, are you pregnant?" she replied, "No John, I am just fat!" I really did want a hole to open and swallow me up, but luckily Henry charged in and gave her a hug to distract her.

Chapter 19
Home Front & Reflection

We had a couple of days in Munster, before being told we could go on leave for five weeks. Jerry Denning, Alistair Ross and I piled into his red Golf GTI 16 valve and headed for Calais. We hit Dover at about 1am and reached London at 2am. We dropped Alistair off at his girlfriends in Clapham and then wanted to get out of the place, as there was a very odd girl there who rather frightened us both. Jerry and I had nowhere to go as both our families were away, so we stopped at a phone box on Clapham Common and I called my old school friend Marcus Hill who lived on Tregavon Road in Clapham. He answered the phone sleepily and asked if I was in Saudi, so I said no Clapham Common and could we have a bed. He said yes and met us at the door with a bottle of champagne. We drank and chatted all night until he had to leave for work. Much of the chat from Marcus was about the amazing 'gun camera' footage from bombers and helicopter gunships, things we had not seen and had no idea what he was talking about as we had no TV in the desert. It did seem a bit odd being told so much about the wider war from someone who saw it all in from his sofa. It made one realise how small our horizon was, mainly at troop and squadron level with the odd sortie up to battle group and never beyond Brigade. Jerry and I slept until midday when Jerry got in touch with his Mum who was back in London, so he left me to slumber at Marcus's and catch up with current affairs on the TV. Marcus came home after what I am sure cannot have been a productive day at the office and told me we had a dinner date in local Italian Restaurant in Clapham. As I walked in I was amazed to see Alistair Crossman, James Hardwick, Hugo Woddis, Ben Wood, Nick Murphy, 'Cheese' Couse and a couple of girls. We had an unbelievable dinner that ended up with me in bed with one of the girls, who would be my girlfriend for a while after that.

As my parents and sister were still away I decided to take up the offer of my soldiers and visit them in Lancashire and Manchester. It was a great trip and I took the train up to Manchester where I was met by Pommers, Leachy and others of my troop and B Squadron. They entertained me royally and I was passed around like a VIP from one family to another being wined, dined and generally spoilt by the parents of my soldiers. It was a humbling experience to meet these wonderful families from all strata of society. All were so welcoming and so extremely kind I was so touched, the boys certainly made sure I saw all of Manchester and the pubs of Lancashire. It was a great rounding off of my experience and a great way to say farewell to my troop as we were to be separated with my departure to Berlin.

On our return to Germany, I had a short time to pack up my room, buy a new car and head off to Berlin where I was appointed Troop Leader 2nd Troop C Squadron, "The Berlin Armoured Squadron". This was a fabulous job and under command of Major Peter Garbutt, one of the very few recipients of any award for the Gulf War in the Regiment. We all felt rather hard done by, as the list of Awards to not only our Regiment, but the whole of the 'Four-gotten Brigade' was a tad short of those received by 7 Brigade and the Rear Echelons. The Commanding Officer, Lt Col Mike Vickery received a well-deserved OBE and for his actions A Squadron Leader, Peter Garbutt got a Mention in Dispatches.

I had put Cpl Simpson up for an award for his actions on the first night of the war, when he continued to fight and engage the enemy after a very close hit that prevented him sending massages on his radios, but he could receive and thus was able to follow my instructions and work into a position to engage the guns in support of me. I also recommended Leechy for a medal for his actions that saved our lives in that first engagement. I know that there were also a number of other citations presented after the war from the Regiment for both our own soldiers but also those of the supporting arms. I am unsure if it was a case that our recommendations were poorly written, presented in the wrong way or if they did not benefit from support further up the chain of command. The net result is demonstrated in the attached table:

I have listed only those in the 1st British Division and then in order Gallantry first and then awards for Service. (SAS and Special Forces awards not included)

Award	7th Armd Brigade	4th Armd Brigade	Division/Support
DSO			Major General Rupert Smith, (Ex-Para)
DSO	Brigadier Patrick Cordingley 7Armd Bgd (Ex-5th RIDG)		
MC	Major Simon Knapper - Staffs		
MC		Major John Potter RHF – Royal Scots	
MC	Major John Rochelle - Staffs		
MC	Acting Major Vincent Maddison - QRIH		
MC		Captain Norman Soutar - RS	
MC		Lieutenant Anthony Guy Briselden – 3RRF	
MC	2nd Lt Richard Telfer - RSDG		

DCM			Staff Sgt Kevin Michael Davies – RMP
MM			Sgt Michael James Dowling – REME ($16^{th}/5^{th}$ L)
MM	Sergeant Nicholas Scott – QRIH		
MM	Cpl Kenneth Anderson - QRIH		
MM		L/Cpl Ian Michael Dewsnap – RE	
MM	L/Cpl Kevin Reid – REME (10 AD RA)		
MM		Pvt Thomas Gow - RS	
AFM			SSGT Mark Torpy – AAC
Total Gallantry In face of Enemy	8	5	4
QGM		Sgt Trevor Smith – 3RRF	
QGM		Pvt Simon Bakkor – 3RRF	
QGM	Sgt Stephen Allen – 10AD RA		
QGM			Cpl Michael Driscoll – RCT Att RAMC
QGM			Corporal Mark Griffiths – REME Att RCT
Total Gallantry Not in face of Enemy	1	2	2

I in no way wish to belittle the amazing acts of bravery that were recognised by the awards given, but feel that there seems to have been some sort of ‘weeding out’ or favouritism shown to the brigade that as far as the tanks were concerned fired far fewer rounds and engaged far fewer targets.

There is no doubt that the Gulf War shaped me in many ways for the future. I grew up a great deal and had a far more realistic approach to life and how I approached problems and difficult people or situations.

Initially I had a complete disregard for anything I felt was trivial. One example of this was when my mother started to fret about getting to her hairdresser on time, so I drove from home to Wells in about 7 minutes, a journey that normally took 20. However this soon developed into a better approach to trivial and mundane matters that gave me a better perspective on life. This change came about after a chat with the father of my old school friend Marcus Hill. Bill Hill had served as the Anti-tank Platoon Commander for 3 Para in Suez. He put my experiences into perspective, something that I think can only be done by someone who has seen combat. Most veterans agree that they most easily relate to those who served with them and then to those who have been in other conflicts. I find this very true.

The other influence was my experiences after the war, when I saw the destruction wrought by the immense firepower at our disposal in a desert. Also the amount of Explosive Remnants of War left in the desert, both our own and the Iraqi. Particularly the mines and cluster bombs. This led me to my career after the army, demining and later to be involved in the cluster bomb ban. It always amazed me that we had a weapon system that seemed so devastatingly effective but could leave such a large legacy, ultimately due to poor design and manufacture. The effects of the MLRS delivered cluster bombs during the war proved to be a devastating weapon, however it also became a liability to us as over 30% did not explode on impact and so acted like anti-personnel mines to us and in particular our infantry. Ironically some of the first casualties of British cluster munitions were the Gunners from 32 Heavy Regiment who fired them and then been told to occupy the very same positions they had just targeted which were littered with unexploded munitions! I was always amazed that the powers-that-be could bring into service a weapon with such a high failure rate. If 30% of what I fired from my tank cannon failed to explode or penetrate the target I would have been up in arms, but there was an acceptance of this failure rate that ultimately led to the banning of an extremely effective weapon system. Had it been designed and produced effectively, cluster bombs would remain in the arsenal of the UK and other armies. As a result of these failures, I became a strong advocate for their banning as they proved to be far more harmful after the wars in which they were used ended.

The war also confirmed my belief that I was not ready to be a soldier for the rest of my life and I left the army in 1993 after probably the most formative seven years in my life. I have never regretted joining the army and never regretted leaving and would recommend it to any young man or woman who wants to start life in possibly one of the best management, leadership and formative institutions in the world.

Annexes

Letters & Telegraph Article

My last bluey before the war:

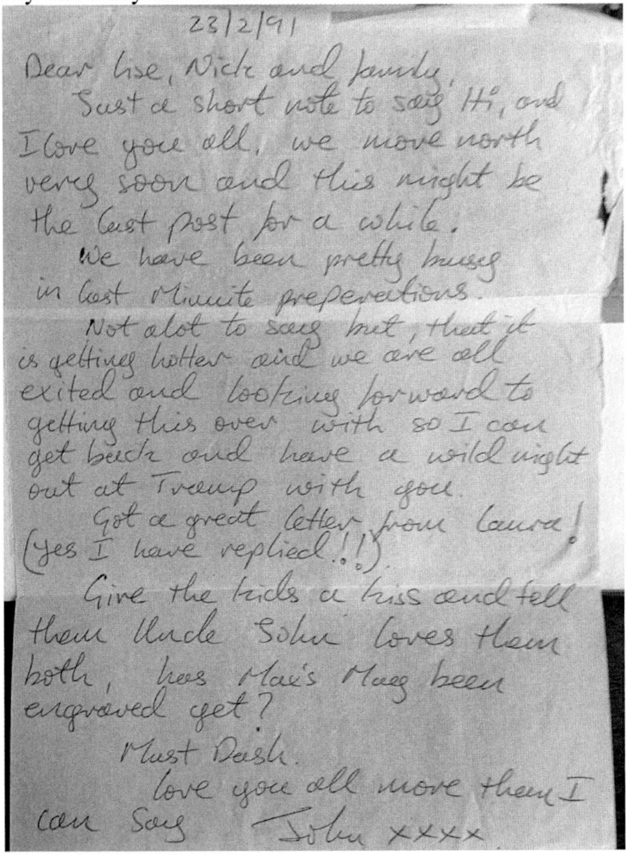

23/2/91

Dear Lise, Nick and family,

Just a short note to say 'Hi', and I love you all, we move north very soon and this might be the last post for a while.

We have been pretty busy in last minute preperations.

Not alot to say but, that it is getting hotter and we are all exited and looking forward to getting this over with so I can get back and have a wild night out at Tramp with you.

Got a great letter from Laura! (yes I have replied!!).

Give the kids a kiss and tell them Uncle John loves them both, has Max's Mug been engraved yet?

Must Dash.

love you all more than I can say John xxxx

Letters from my soldiers parents to my parents in response to their letter to them with a photo of each tank crew:

Trp. Hindmoor parents' letter

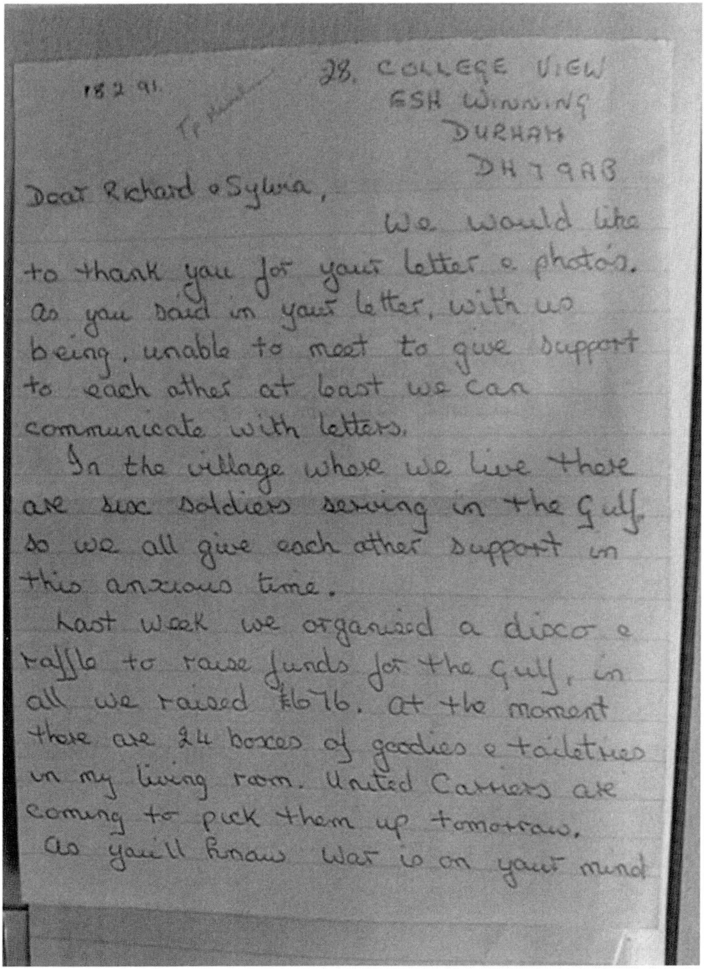

18.2.91.

28, COLLEGE VIEW
ESH WINNING
DURHAM
DH7 9AB

Dear Richard & Sylvia,

We would like to thank you for your letter & photo's. as you said in your letter, with us being, unable to meet to give support to each other at least we can communicate with letters.

In the village where we live there are six soldiers serving in the Gulf. so we all give each other support in this anxious time.

Last week we organised a disco & raffle to raise funds for the Gulf, in all we raised £676. at the moment there are 24 boxes of goodies & toiletries in my living room. United Carriers are coming to pick them up tomorrow.

As you'll know War is on your mind

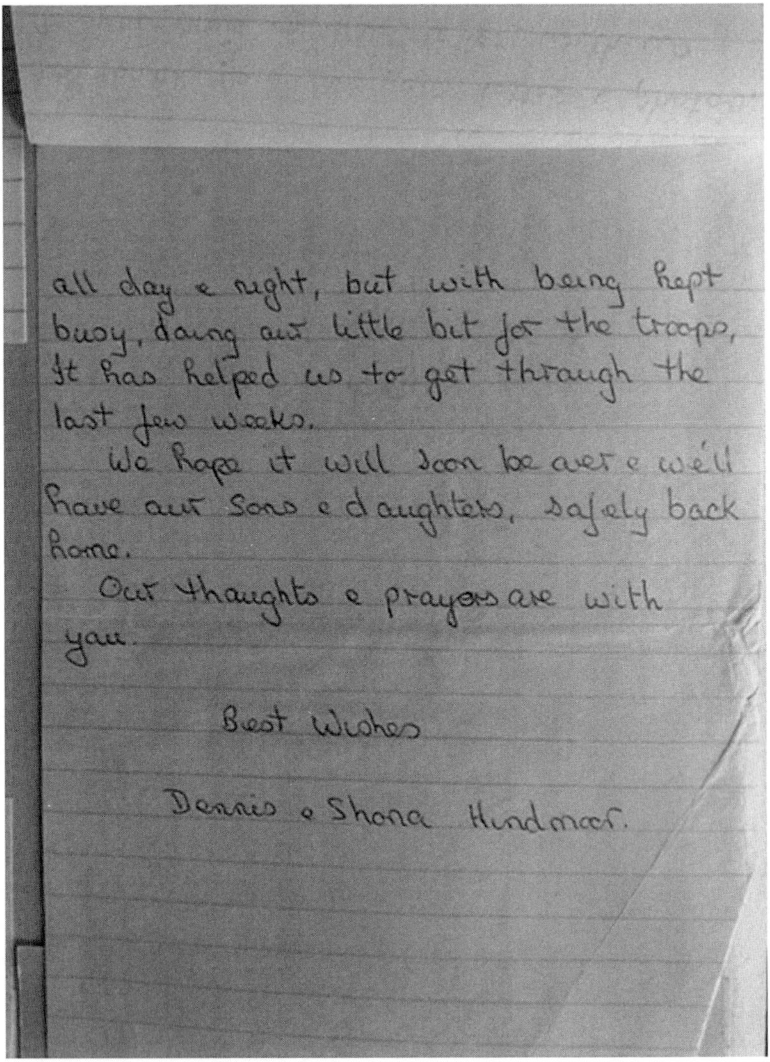

all day & night, but with being kept busy, doing our little bit for the troops, It has helped us to get through the last few weeks.

We hope it will soon be over & we'll have our sons & daughters, safely back home.

Our thoughts & prayers are with you.

Best Wishes

Dennis & Shona Hindmoor.

Trooper Woolstonholm's parent's letter.

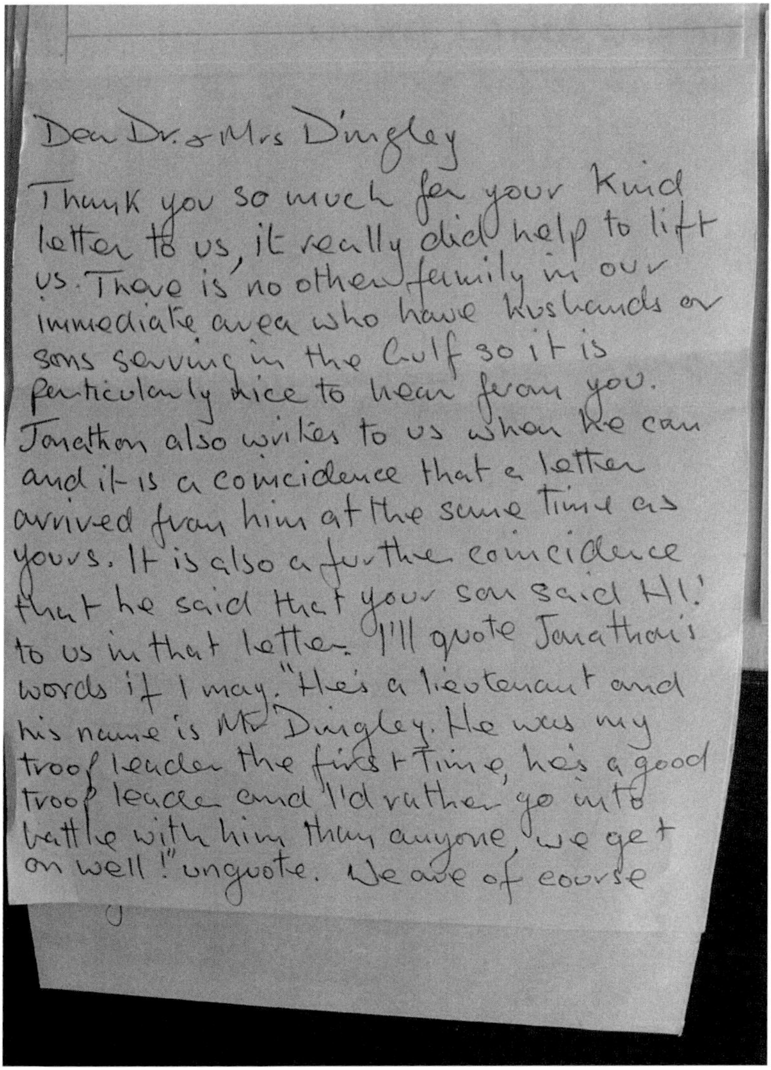
Dear Dr. & Mrs Dingley

Thank you so much for your kind letter to us, it really did help to lift us. There is no other family in our immediate area who have husbands or sons serving in the Gulf so it is particularly nice to hear from you. Jonathon also writes to us when he can and it is a coincidence that a letter arrived from him at the same time as yours. It is also a further coincidence that he said that your son said HI! to us in that letter. I'll quote Jonathan's words if I may. "He's a lieutenant and his name is Mr Dingley. He was my troop leader the first time, he's a good troop leader and I'd rather go into battle with him than anyone, we get on well!" unquote. We are of course

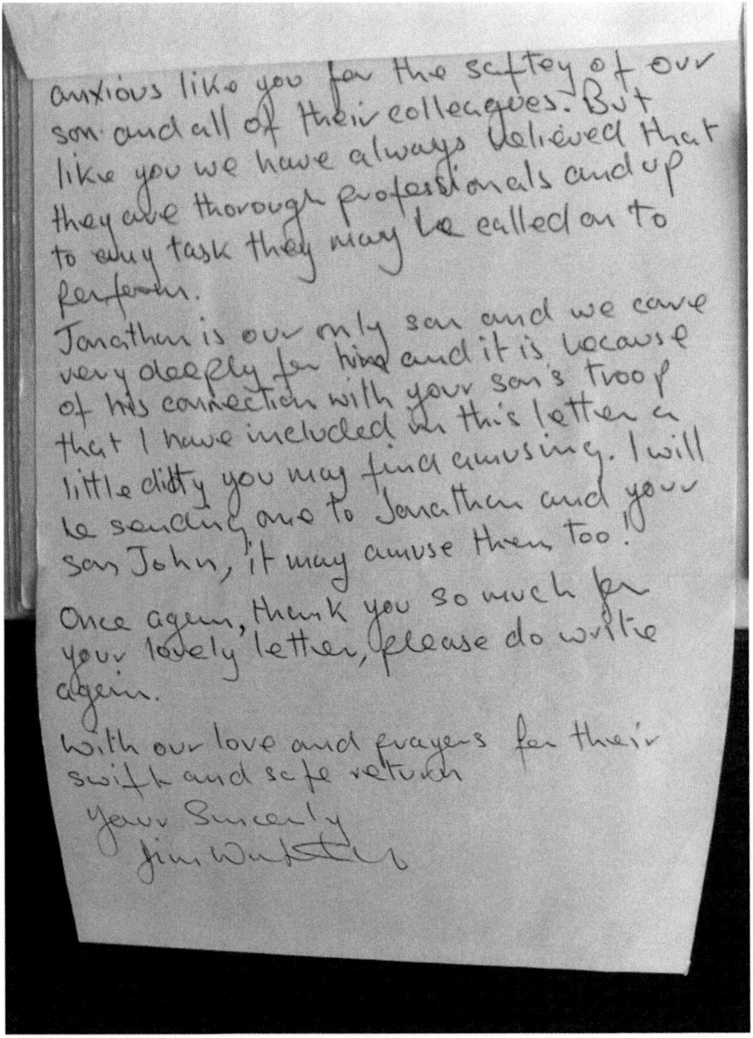

anxious like you for the saftey of our son and all of their colleagues. But like you we have always believed that they are thorough professionals and up to any task they may be called on to perform.

Jonathan is our only son and we care very deeply for him and it is because of his connection with your son's troop that I have included in this letter a little ditty you may find amusing. I will be sending one to Jonathan and your son John, it may amuse them too!

Once again, thank you so much for your lovely letter, please do write again.

With our love and prayers for their swift and safe return

Yours Sincerely

Jim W[illegible]

Sergeant Milner's wife's letter

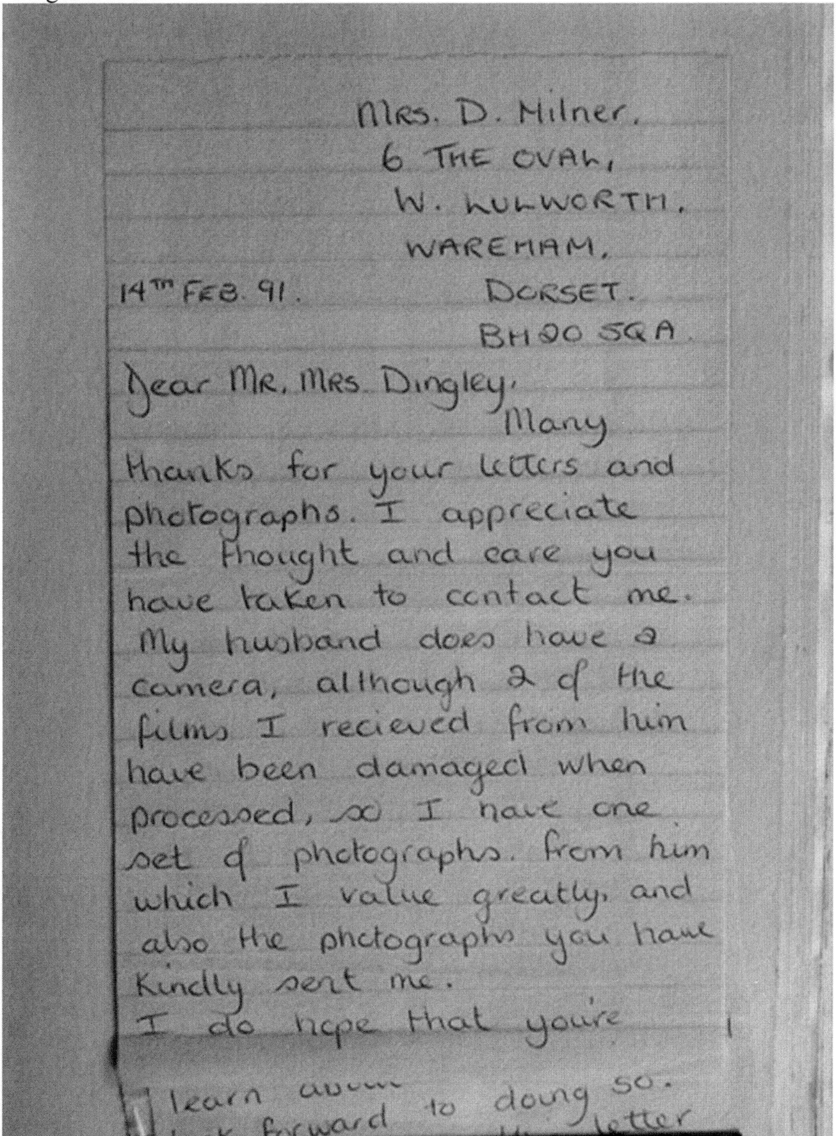

MRS. D. MILNER.
6 THE OVAL,
W. LULWORTH.
WAREHAM.
DORSET.
BH20 5QA.

14TH FEB. 91.

Dear Mr. Mrs Dingley,

Many thanks for your letters and photographs. I appreciate the thought and care you have taken to contact me. My husband does have a camera, although 2 of the films I recieved from him have been damaged when processed, so I have one set of photographs from him which I value greatly, and also the photographs you have kindly sent me.

I do hope that you're

learn [illegible] to doing so.
[illegible] forward [illegible] letter

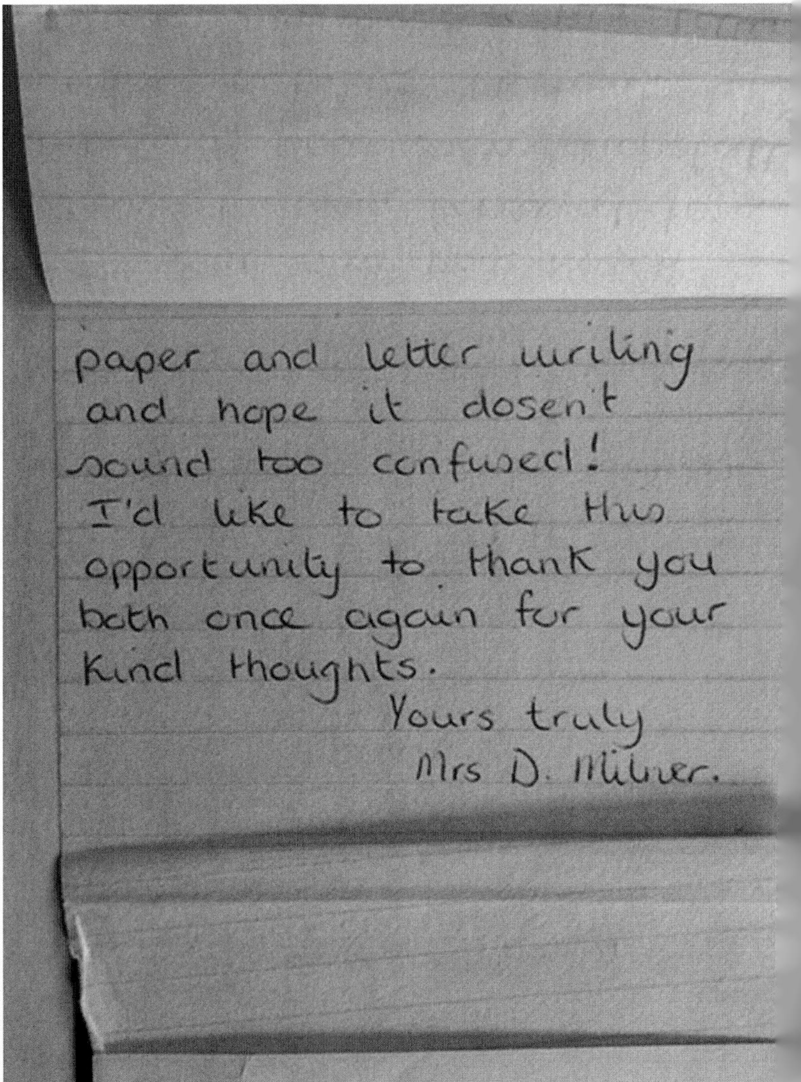

paper and letter writing
and hope it dosen't
sound too confused!
I'd like to take this
opportunity to thank you
both once again for your
kind thoughts.

Yours truly
Mrs D. Milner.

Lance Corporal Pomfret's parent's letter

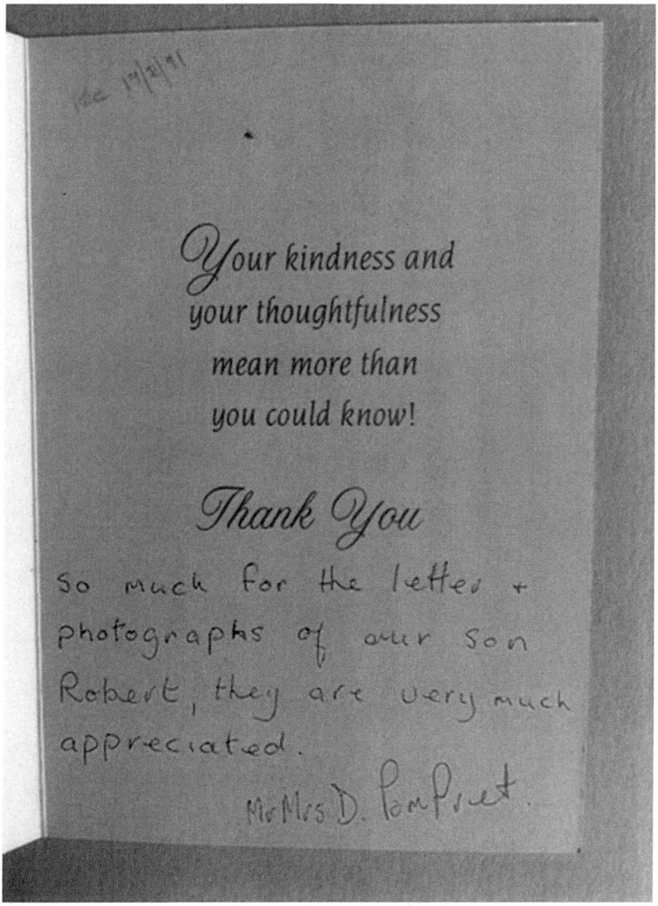

Rec 17/2/91

Your kindness and
your thoughtfulness
mean more than
you could know!

Thank You

so much for the letter + photographs of our son Robert, they are very much appreciated.

Mr Mrs D. Pomfret.

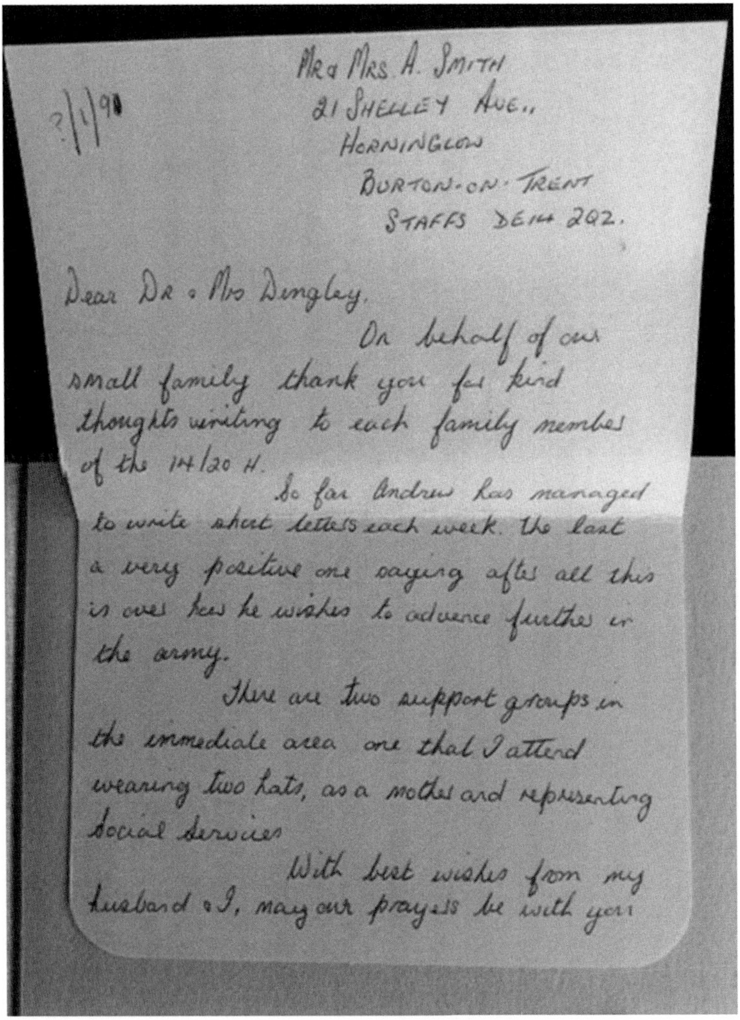

7/1/91

Mr & Mrs. A. Smith
21 Shelley Ave.,
Horninglow
Burton-on-Trent
Staffs DE14 2QZ.

Dear Dr & Mrs Dingley,

On behalf of our small family thank you for kind thoughts writing to each family member of the 14/20 H.

So far Andrew has managed to write short letters each week. the last a very positive one saying after all this is over how he wishes to advance further in the army.

There are two support groups in the immediate area one that I attend wearing two hats, as a mother and representing Social Services

With best wishes from my husband & I, may our prayers be with you

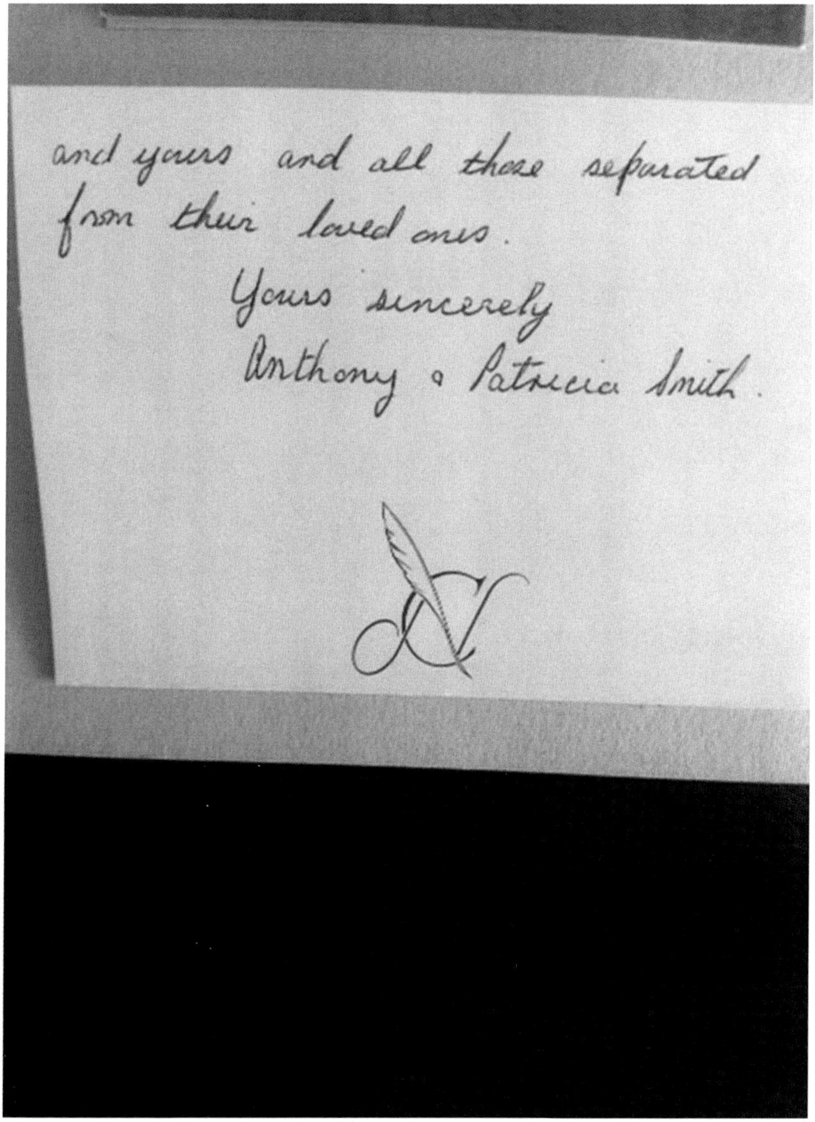
and yours and all those separated
from their loved ones.
Yours sincerely
Anthony & Patricia Smith.

Trooper Hopkins' parent's letter

Mr & Mrs F. Hopkins,
46 Eskdale Street,
Peat Carr Estate,
Hetton-le-Hole,
Tyne & Wear,
DH5 0BL.

7th February 1991

Dear Mr & Mrs Dingley,

On behalf of the two of us and our family I would like to thank you for your letter. It is a great comfort to hear such words from your son John and I salute what I think shows his great character, please thank him.

My son Wayne is the eldest of three boys and has four sisters, so he has quite a few immediate family thinking of him daily.

The last letter we received from our son was delivered on 2nd February, from that letter Wayne appears to be of high spirit and seems to have retained his sense of humour and speaks well of his comrades and of their equipment.

Once again "thank you" for your kind words and thoughts and I join you in prayers for their safe return.

Yours sincerely,

Fred and Jennifer Hopkins

Trooper Miles's parents' letter

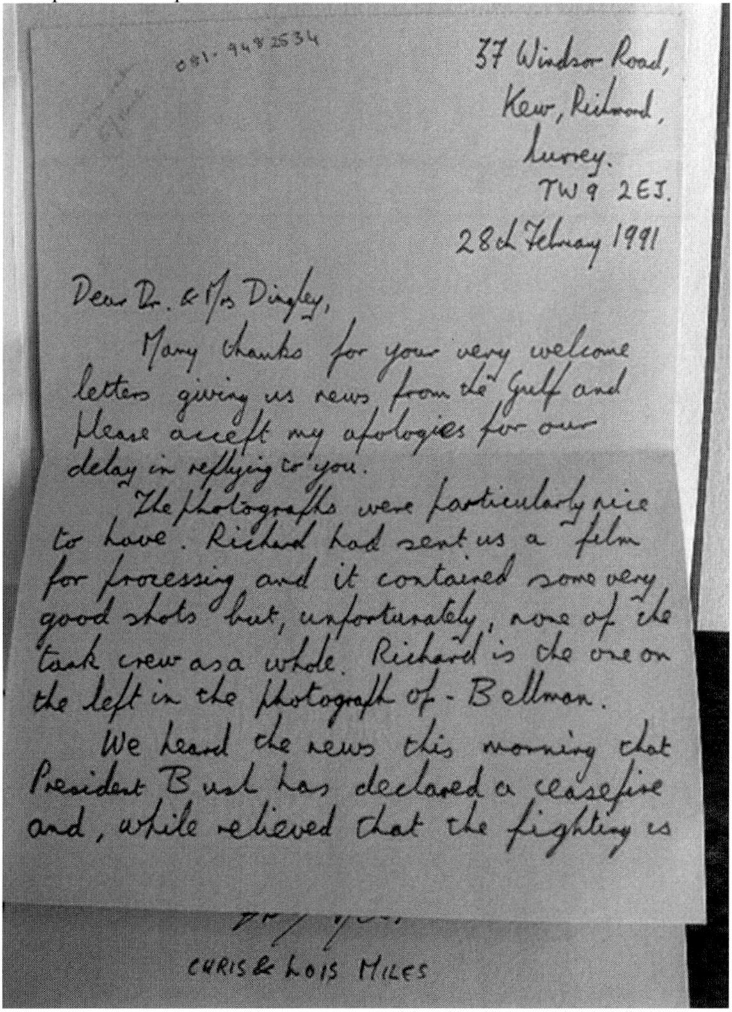

081-948 2534

37 Windsor Road,
Kew, Richmond,
Surrey.
TW9 2EJ.

28th February 1991

Dear Dr. & Mrs Dingley,

Many thanks for your very welcome letters giving us news from the Gulf and please accept my apologies for our delay in replying to you.

The photographs were particularly nice to have. Richard had sent us a film for processing and it contained some very good shots but, unfortunately, none of the tank crew as a whole. Richard is the one on the left in the photograph of - Bellman.

We heard the news this morning that President Bush has declared a ceasefire and, while relieved that the fighting is

CHRIS & LOIS MILES

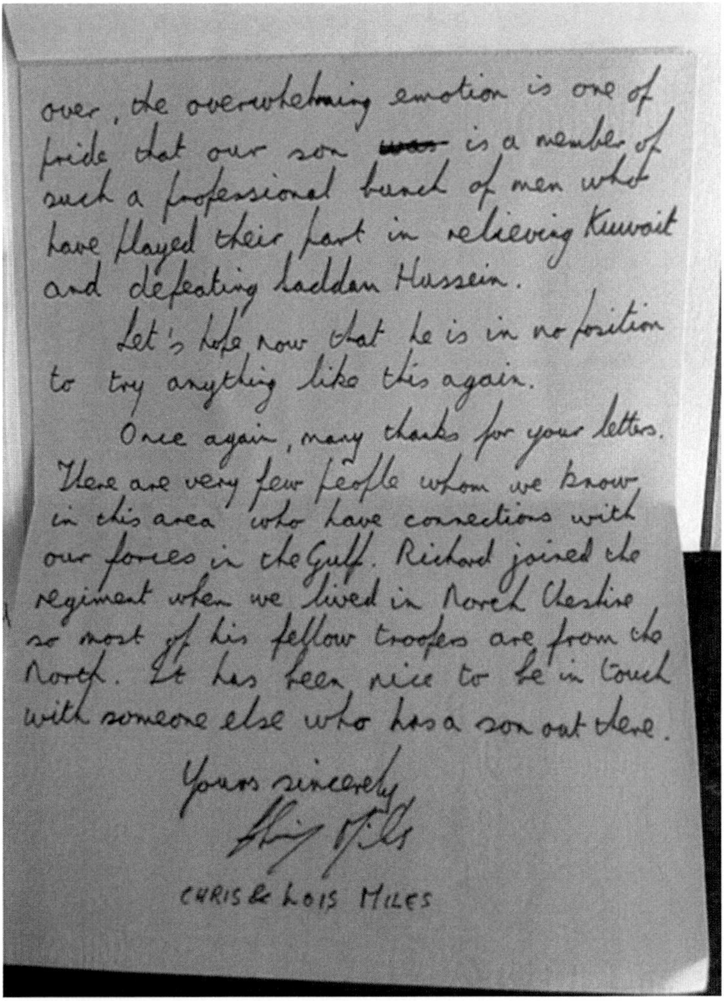

over, the overwhelming emotion is one of pride that our son ~~was~~ is a member of such a professional bunch of men who have played their part in relieving Kuwait and defeating Saddam Hussein.

Let's hope now that he is in no position to try anything like this again.

Once again, many thanks for your letters. There are very few people whom we know in this area who have connections with our forces in the Gulf. Richard joined the regiment when we lived in North Cheshire so most of his fellow troopers are from the North. It has been nice to be in touch with someone else who has a son out there.

Yours sincerely

[illegible]

CHRIS & LOIS MILES

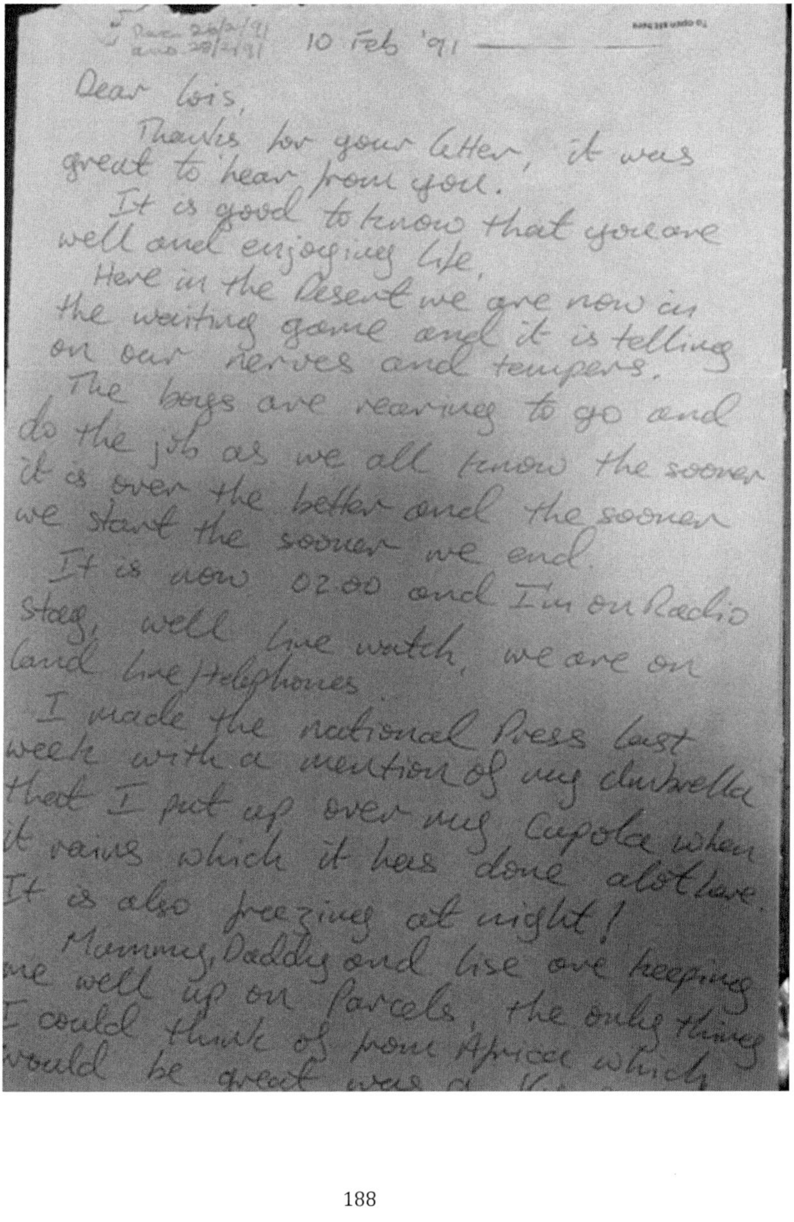

10 Feb '91

Dear Lois,

Thanks for your letter, it was great to hear from you.

It is good to know that you are well and enjoying life.

Here in the Desert we are now in the waiting game and it is telling on our nerves and tempers.

The boys are rearing to go and do the job as we all know the sooner it is over the better and the sooner we start the sooner we end.

It is now 02:00 and I'm on Radio Stag, well line watch, we are on land line telephones.

I made the national Press last week with a mention of my umbrella that I put up over my Cupola when it rains which it has done alot here.

It is also freezing at night!

Mammy, Daddy and Lise are keeping me well up on Parcels, the only thing I could think of from Africa which would be great was a

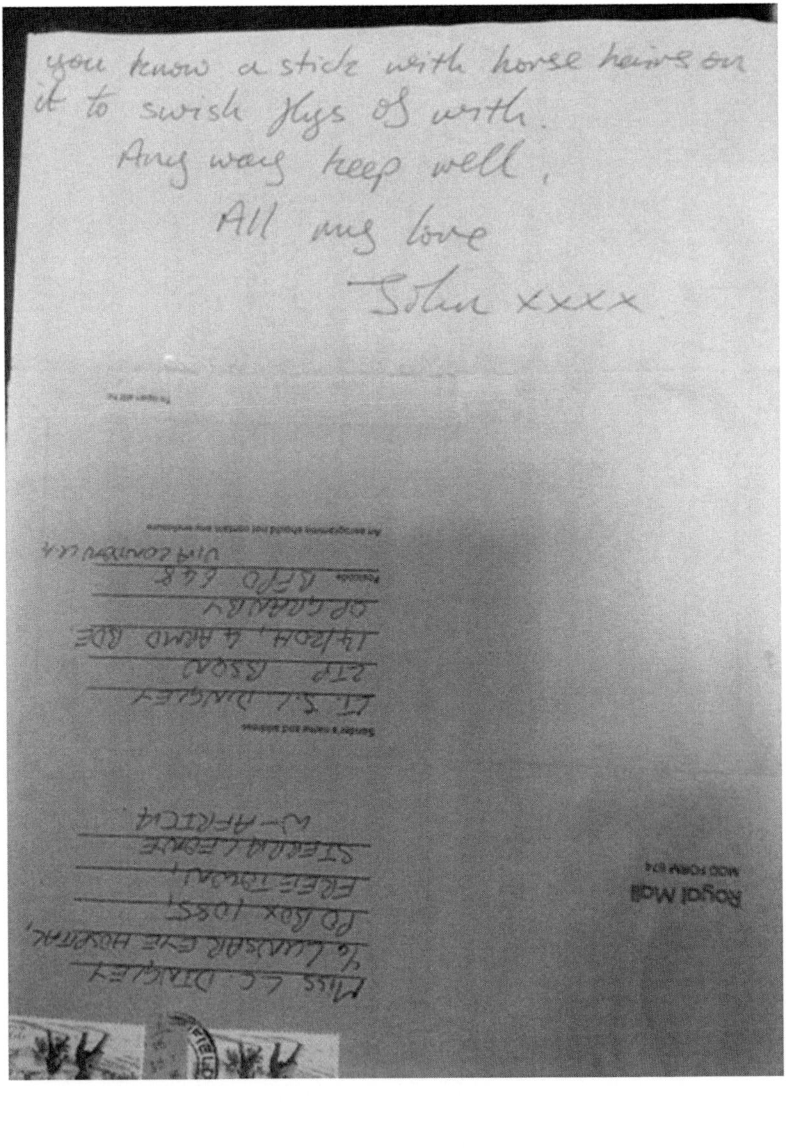
you know a stick with horse hairs on
it to swish flys off with.
Any way keep well,
All my love
John xxxx

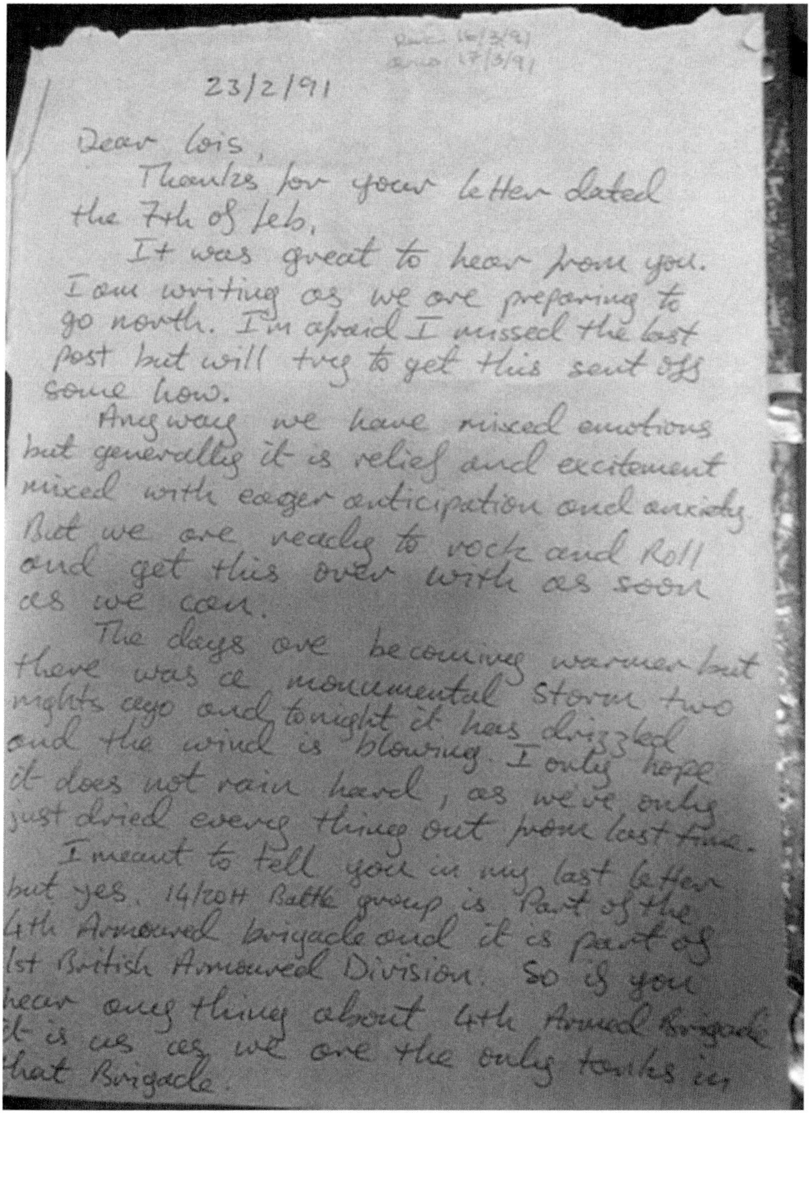

16/3/91
17/3/91

23/2/91

Dear Lois,

Thanks for your letter dated the 7th of Feb.

It was great to hear from you. I am writing as we are preparing to go north. I'm afraid I missed the last post but will try to get this sent off some how.

Anyway we have mixed emotions but generally it is relief and excitement mixed with eager anticipation and anxiety. But we are ready to rock and Roll and get this over with as soon as we can.

The days are becoming warmer but there was a monumental storm two nights ago and tonight it has drizzled and the wind is blowing. I only hope it does not rain hard, as we've only just dried every thing out from last time.

I meant to tell you in my last letter but yes. 14/20H Battle group is Part of the 4th Armoured brigade and it is part of 1st British Armoured Division. So if you hear any thing about 4th Armd Brigade it is us as we are the only tanks in that Brigade.

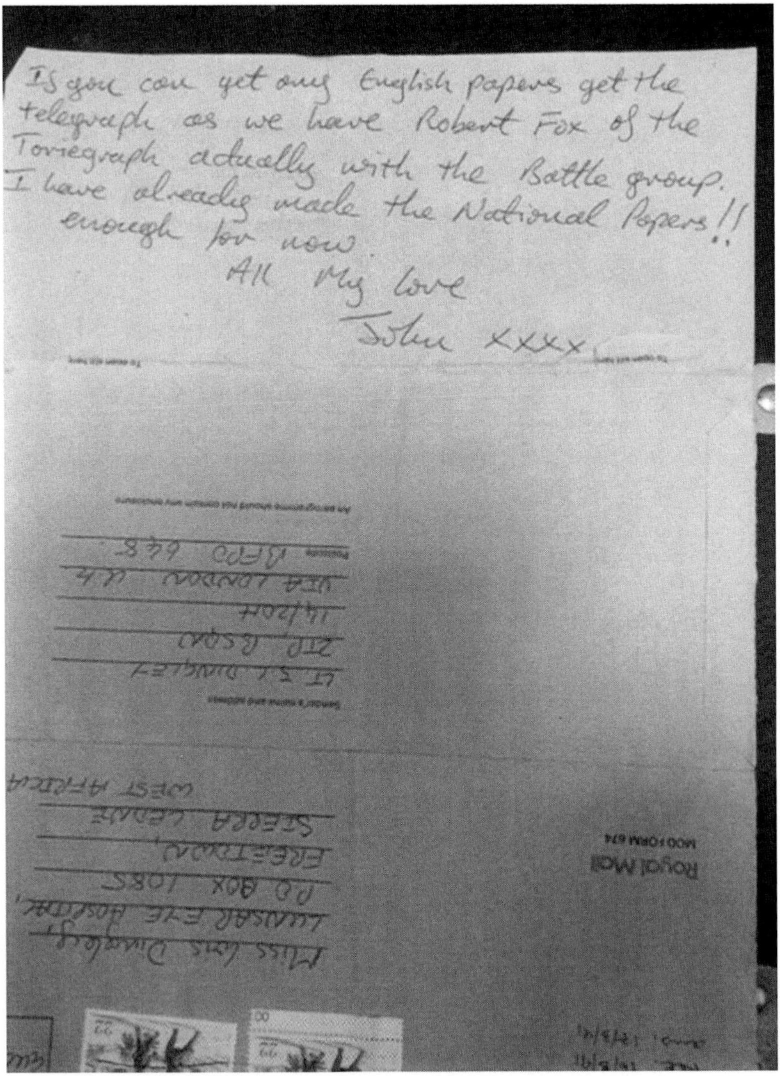

If you can get any English papers get the
telegraph as we have Robert Fox of the
Toriegraph actually with the Battle group.
I have already made the National Papers!!
enough for now.
All My love
John xxxx.

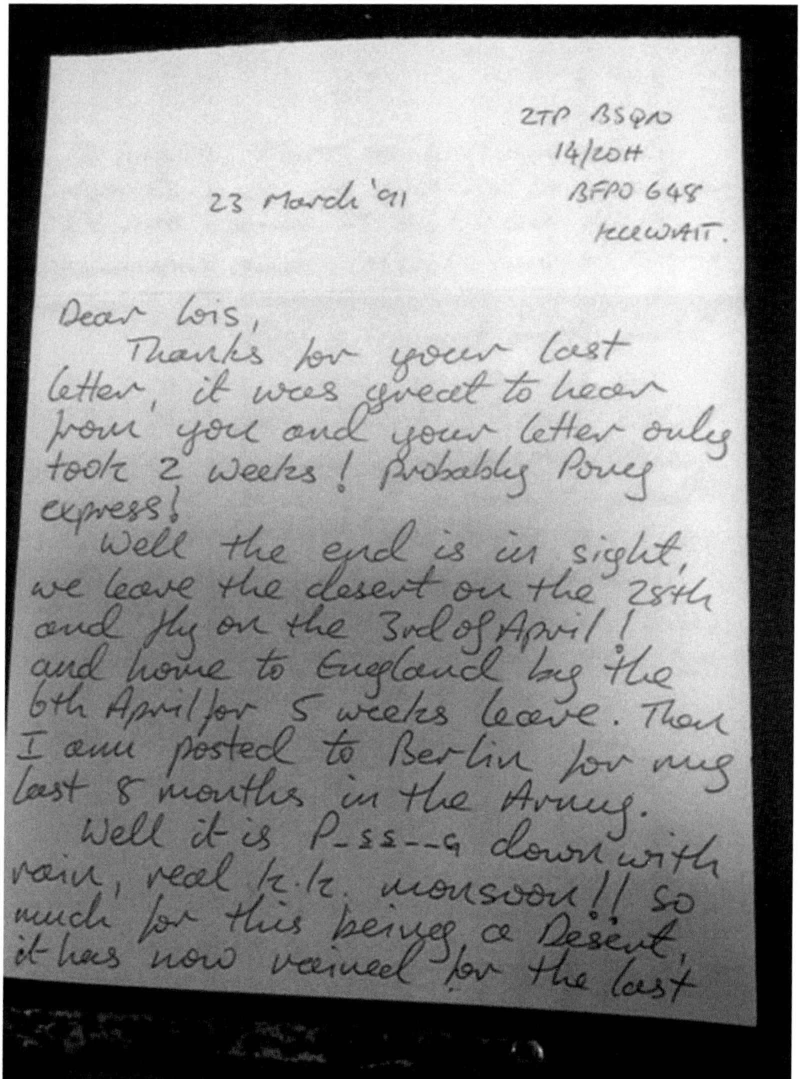

2TP BSQN
14/20H
BFPO 648
KUWAIT.

23 March '91

Dear Lois,

Thanks for your last letter, it was great to hear from you and your letter only took 2 weeks! Probably Pony express!

Well the end is in sight, we leave the desert on the 28th and fly on the 3rd of April! and home to England by the 6th April for 5 weeks leave. Then I am posted to Berlin for my last 8 months in the Army.

Well it is P_ss__g down with rain, real k.k. monsoon!! So much for this being a Desert, it has now rained for the last

(2)

18 hours, More rain than any records since we arrived in December. We are going to build an ARK tomorrow and collect two of every thing! We did a great battle field tour with some Yanks in a U.S. helocopter and I saw what we did in day light and how much we came up against, And what nearly hit my tank on the first contact. It was a battery of 3 MT 12 100mm anti tank Guns. had we not moved after the 1st shot we would have been hit. Now it blows my mind just thinking about it.

Other than that life here goes on and we are very bored so there is little to write about

So bye for Now

Lots of Love John xx xx

Pen Pal Letter

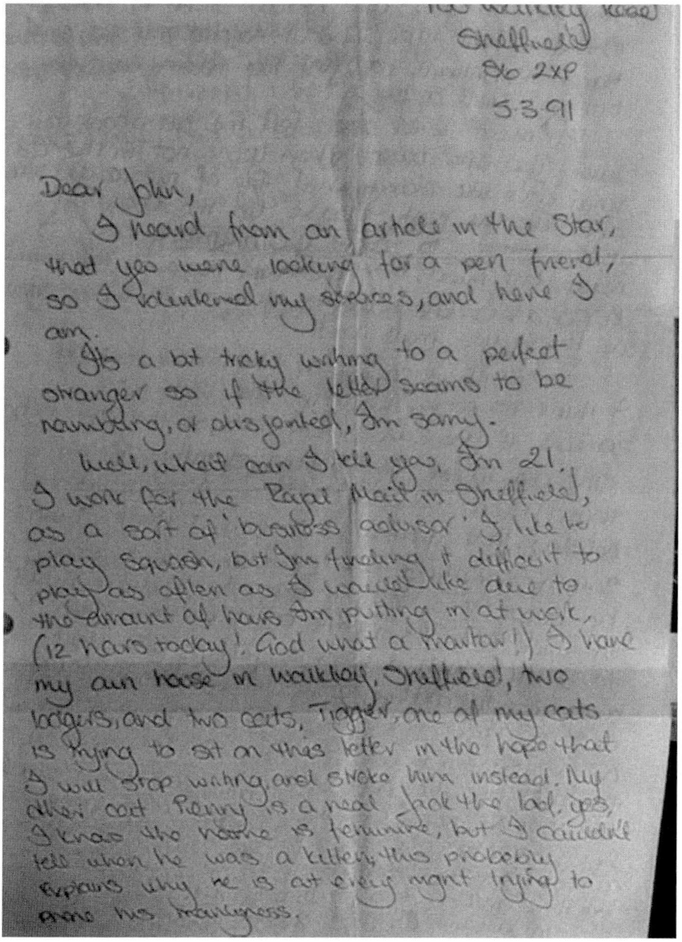

[illegible] Walkley Road
Sheffield
S6 2XP

5.3.91

Dear John,

I heard from an article in the Star, that you were looking for a pen friend, so I volunteered my services, and here I am.

It's a bit tricky writing to a perfect stranger so if the letter seems to be rambling, or disjointed, I'm sorry.

Well, what can I tell you, I'm 21, I work for the Royal Mail in Sheffield, as a sort of 'business advisor'. I like to play squash, but I'm finding it difficult to play as often as I would like due to the amount of hours I'm putting in at work, (12 hours today! God what a martyr!) I have my own house in Walkley, Sheffield, two lodgers, and two cats, Tigger, one of my cats is trying to sit on this letter in the hope that I will stop writing and stroke him instead. My other cat Penny is a real Jack the lad, yes, I know the name is feminine, but I couldn't tell when he was a kitten, this probably explains why he is out every night trying to prove his manliness.

Robert Fox's Umbrella Article

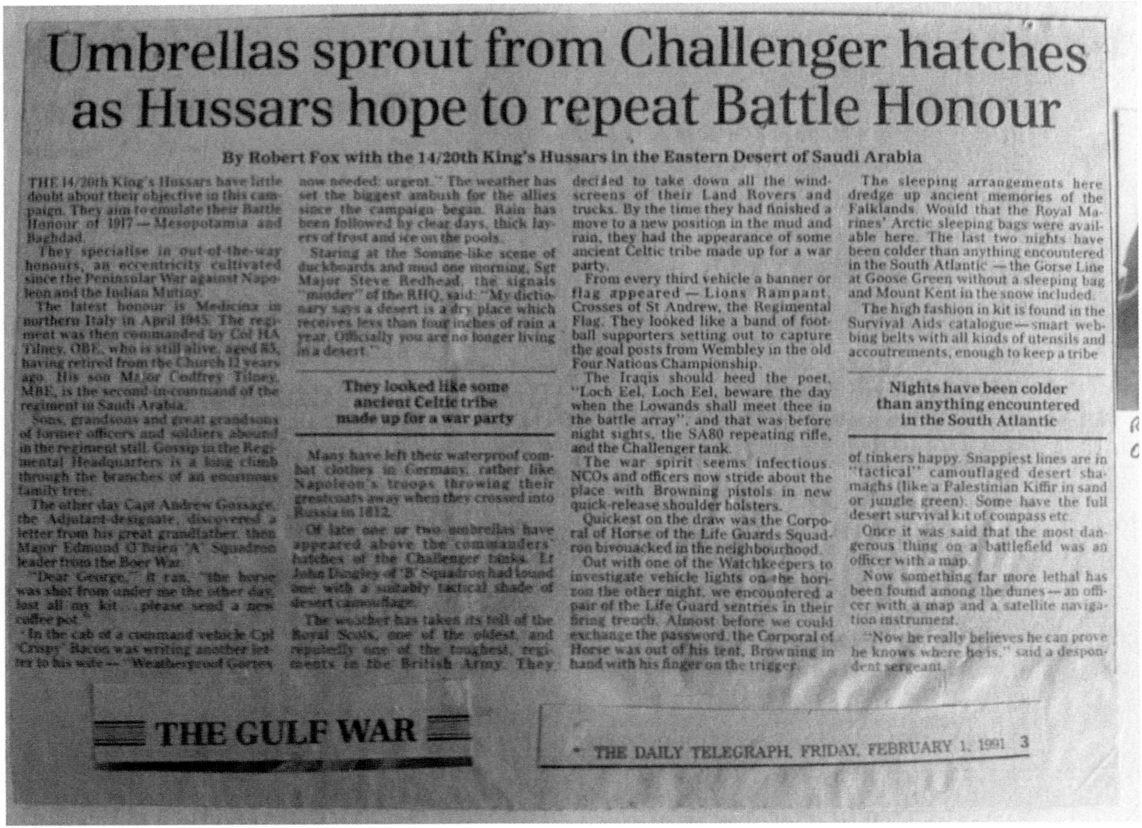

Umbrellas sprout from Challenger hatches as Hussars hope to repeat Battle Honour

By Robert Fox with the 14/20th King's Hussars in the Eastern Desert of Saudi Arabia

THE 14/20th King's Hussars have little doubt about their objective in this campaign. They aim to emulate their Battle Honour of 1917 — Mesopotamia and Baghdad.

They specialise in out-of-the-way honours, an eccentricity cultivated since the Peninsular War against Napoleon and the Indian Mutiny.

The latest honour is Medicina in northern Italy in April 1945. The regiment was then commanded by Col HA Tilney, OBE, who is still alive, aged 85, having retired from the Church 12 years ago. His son Major Godfrey Tilney, MBE, is the second-in-command of the regiment in Saudi Arabia.

Sons, grandsons and great grandsons of former officers and soldiers abound in the regiment still. Gossip in the Regimental Headquarters is a long climb through the branches of an enormous family tree.

The other day Capt Andrew Gossage, the Adjutant-designate, discovered a letter from his great grandfather, then Major Edmund O'Brien 'A' Squadron leader from the Boer War.

"Dear George," it ran, "the horse was shot from under me the other day, lost all my kit ... please send a new coffee pot."

In the cab of a command vehicle Cpl "Crispy" Bacon was writing another letter to his wife — "Weatherproof Gortex now needed: urgent." The weather has set the biggest ambush for the allies since the campaign began. Rain has been followed by clear days, thick layers of frost and ice on the pools.

Staring at the Somme-like scene of duckboards and mud one morning, Sgt Major Steve Redhead, the signals "minder" of the RHQ, said: "My dictionary says a desert is a dry place which receives less than four inches of rain a year. Officially you are no longer living in a desert."

They looked like some ancient Celtic tribe made up for a war party

Many have left their waterproof combat clothes in Germany, rather like Napoleon's troops throwing their greatcoats away when they crossed into Russia in 1812.

Of late one or two umbrellas have appeared above the commanders' hatches of the Challenger tanks. Lt John Dingley of 'B' Squadron had found one with a suitably tactical shade of desert camouflage.

The weather has taken its toll of the Royal Scots, one of the oldest, and reputedly one of the toughest, regiments in the British Army. They decided to take down all the windscreens of their Land Rovers and trucks. By the time they had finished a move to a new position in the mud and rain, they had the appearance of some ancient Celtic tribe made up for a war party.

From every third vehicle a banner or flag appeared — Lions Rampant, Crosses of St Andrew, the Regimental Flag. They looked like a band of football supporters setting out to capture the goal posts from Wembley in the old Four Nations Championship.

The Iraqis should heed the poet, "Loch Eel, Loch Eel, beware the day when the Lowands shall meet thee in the battle array", and that was before night sights, the SA80 repeating rifle, and the Challenger tank.

The war spirit seems infectious. NCOs and officers now stride about the place with Browning pistols in new quick-release shoulder holsters.

Quickest on the draw was the Corporal of Horse of the Life Guards Squadron bivouacked in the neighbourhood.

Out with one of the Watchkeepers to investigate vehicle lights on the horizon the other night, we encountered a pair of the Life Guard sentries in their firing trench. Almost before we could exchange the password, the Corporal of Horse was out of his tent, Browning in hand with his finger on the trigger.

The sleeping arrangements here dredge up ancient memories of the Falklands. Would that the Royal Marines' Arctic sleeping bags were available here. The last two nights have been colder than anything encountered in the South Atlantic — the Gorse Line at Goose Green without a sleeping bag and Mount Kent in the snow included.

The high fashion in kit is found in the Survival Aids catalogue — smart webbing belts with all kinds of utensils and accoutrements, enough to keep a tribe of tinkers happy. Snappiest lines are in "tactical" camouflaged desert shamaghs (like a Palestinian Kiffir in sand or jungle green). Some have the full desert survival kit of compass etc.

Nights have been colder than anything encountered in the South Atlantic

Once it was said that the most dangerous thing on a battlefield was an officer with a map.

Now something far more lethal has been found among the dunes — an officer with a map and a satellite navigation instrument.

"Now he really believes he can prove he knows where he is," said a despondent sergeant.

THE GULF WAR

THE DAILY TELEGRAPH, FRIDAY, FEBRUARY 1, 1991 3

About the Author

John Dingley was brought up in Sabah, East Malaysia and educated in the UK at The Downs School, Colwall and Uppingham School, Rutland. After a brief year at City of London Polytechnic trying to study geology he gave up and worked as a skiing instructor in Norway before entering the Royal Military Academy Sandhurst graduating on 12th December 1986. He joined the 14th/20th Kings Hussars in Catterick where he trained recruits after attending his Armoured Tank Commanders and Troop Leaders course at Bovington.

He then served in a number of countries and postings both with the regiment in Munster, Northern Ireland, Canada, Norway and attached to the Blues and Royals in Sennelager, Germany and finally with the 1st Battalion The Light Infantry in Belize.

Leaving the Army in 1993, he embarked on a career in humanitarian demining, starting with HALO Trust in Mozambique and then working with a number of International Non-Governmental Organisations and commercial companies in Mozambique, Iraqi Kurdistan, Angola, Bosnia and Cambodia. He then joined the United Nations where he worked with the United Nations Development Programme Mine Action Unit for twelve years in Somalia, Lao PDR & Yemen with a brief eighteen months in South Sudan with the United Nations Mine Action Service. In 2014 he left UNDP Mine Action and moved to The World Food Programme as a security officer.

John is married to Katrina with three sons and is based out of Kenya.